MW00780036

Tuskegee Airmen

Tuskegee Airmen

DOGFIGHTING WITH THE LUFTWAFFE AND JIM CROW

SAMUEL de KORTE

AIR WORLD

AIR WORLD

TUSKEGEE AIRMEN
Dogfighting with the Luftwaffe and Jim Crow

First published in Great Britain in 2024 by
Pen & Sword Air World
An imprint of
Pen & Sword Books Ltd
Yorkshire – Philadelphia

ISBN 978 1 39904 381 6

Typeset by SJmagic DESIGN SERVICES, India.

Printed and bound in the UK by CPI Group (UK) Ltd.

Pen & Sword Books Ltd. incorporates the Imprints of Pen & Sword Archaeology, Atlas, Aviation, Battleground, Discovery, Family History, History, Maritime, Military, Naval, Politics, Railways, Select, Transport, True Crime, Fiction, Frontline Books, Leo Cooper, Praetorian Press, Seaforth Publishing, Wharncliffe, White Owl and After the Battle.

For a complete list of Pen & Sword titles please contact

PEN & SWORD BOOKS LIMITED
George House, Units 12 & 13, Beevor Street, Off Pontefract Road,
Barnsley, South Yorkshire, S71 1HN, England
E-mail: enquiries@pen-and-sword.co.uk
Website: www.pen-and-sword.co.uk

or

PEN AND SWORD BOOKS
1950 Lawrence Rd, Havertown, PA 19083, USA
E-mail: uspen-and-sword@casematepublishers.com
Website: www.penandswordbooks.com

Contents

Foreword

In the 1940s, psychologists Kenneth and Mamie Clark conducted a series of experiments on Black children. The purpose of these experiments was to study the psychological effects of segregation on Black American children. In this experiment four dolls were presented to the children and questions were asked about the dolls. The four dolls were identical, except for color, with two dolls being described as white and two dolls being described as black. The majority of the children preferred the white dolls and assumed positive characteristics about them, such as it being "nice", while negative characteristics were assigned to the black dolls, such as it being "bad".

In his paper, Kenneth Clark concluded that segregation solely on the basis of race caused a feeling of inferiority in Black American children, that racism was an inherently American institution and that segregation repressed the development of white children as well. The research was presented as evidence in a Supreme Court case, Brown v. Board, which ruled in 1954 that racial segregation was unconstitutional. "Separate-but-equal" was often "separate-and-unequal". From this moment on, education would be integrated.

Just like education, so too does history need to be integrated. The diversity of the past needs to be acknowledged. Although Black Americans formed around 10 per cent of the American army during the Second World War, they do not receive 10 per cent of the attention of the contemporary media. Their contribution is often ignored or forgotten in books or movies, despite the services they performed.

Due to the reigning prejudices about Black Americans during the Second World War, most of the Black soldiers were relegated to support roles. They would load and unload the ships that carried white soldiers across the sea, or drive the trucks that carried these white soldiers to the battlefield, and return with white casualties, which would either be delivered to an aid-station or prepared for burial, the latter service also often performed by Black American soldiers.

Yet Black American soldiers fought on all fronts during the Second World War. There were the 92nd and 93rd Infantry Division, the 761st, 758th, 784th Tank Battalions, the 614th Tank Destroyer Battalion, the 333rd, 578th, 686th, 777th, 969th, and the 999th Field Artillery Battalion, and the 452nd Anti-Aircraft Artillery Battalion to name a few units. Even Black women served, such as the 6888th Central Postal Directory Battalion.

The most well-known Black American unit that participated in the Second World War was the 332nd Fighter Group, also known as the "Red Tails", due to the red markings on the rear of the plane. These pilots are also called the Tuskegee Airmen. While all of the "Red Tails" were Tuskegee Airmen, the term also applies to Black American pilots that were trained and served in a variety of other roles, such as artillery liaisons or the bomber crews. On the ground, mechanics, nurses, and a host of support staff ensured that the fighters could take off and the fighter group operated as it should. They, too, are Tuskegee Airmen.

In the following pages, you will read about these inspiring heroes, men and women that endured despite all odds, and the efforts they made to get there. In the past a variety of methods were employed to prevent these American heroes from achieving their goals. This could be, but is not limited to, verbal violence. Such quotes are present in the text. Black Americans at that time endured it and to remove or alter the abuse that they endured would both diminish their achievement, as well as give the suggestion that the abuse was not such an issue after all. If this offends a contemporary audience, I apologize in advance.

As in regards to the use of the source material, so too has a decision been made in the presentation of this research. The discussion is still ongoing and with the passage of time, ideas about capitalization may change and another choice might be made in the future. Ethnicity and race are oft-debated topics in the US and elsewhere. Regarding their capitalization, the choice has been made in this text to capitalize Black, but not white. Capitalizing Black is an acknowledgment of the shared history and culture of Black Americans, whereas this does not always

FOREWORD

apply in the same way to white Americans. Furthermore, I would not wish to lend any credibility to white supremacists, which is the opposite of what this book tries to achieve. Thus, the decision is made to use Black and white throughout the book.

Since its establishment, the United States Air Force went by several names. In 1918 it was formed as the United States Army Air Service. The US Army Air Corps, as it was known in 1926, became the US Army Air Forces in 1941. In 1947 it would change its name again, becoming the United States Air Force.

Lastly, a word of thanks to you the reader, because you're keeping the history of the Tuskegee Airmen alive.

Chapter 1

Pre-Second World War

The First World War

On 6 April 1917 the United States of America officially declared war on the German Empire and actively joined the First World War. At the beginning of 1917 the German Empire had resumed its attacks on American merchant ships. Later, the Zimmerman Telegram, in which the German Empire proposed to Mexico an alliance in case the United States declared war on the German Empire, was intercepted by British Intelligence and passed along to the US government. A declaration of war from the United States against the German Empire followed shortly afterwards.

At that time, in war-torn Western Europe, the battle on the ground had become a stalemate with French and British soldiers entrenched on one side and the German soldiers on the other side. Both sides were firmly dug in and the front wavered little from the previous years. Meanwhile, the battle had also taken to the skies. Airplanes had been a relatively new invention and initially been used for reconnaissance purposes. Since anti-aircraft warfare was in its infancy, the best way to prevent aerial reconnaissance was to engage the airplanes with other aircraft.[1]

Once the US entered the war, a Black American pilot, Eugene Bullard, tried to enlist in the Air Service of the American Expeditionary Force. In the previous years he had fought as a soldier in the French Army and was later trained as an air gunner and pilot. However, as he described in his own words:

> I was more and more puzzled until suddenly it came to me that all my fellow countrymen who were transferred were white. Later I learned that in World War I, Negroes

1

were not accepted as fliers by the US Army. This hurt me very much. Then as now, my love for my country was strong.[2]

Although the US was at war, they denied Black pilots the chance to serve, and refused to train Black pilots. Black American soldiers of the 93rd Infantry Division were put under French command, so they would not serve alongside white American soldiers. The tone for the following years was set. Black soldiers could serve, but they were largely relegated to support roles and in segregated units.

Eugene Bullard besides a Nieuport while with Escadrille 93 (Public Domain)

Eugene Bullard, however, was not the only Black person to fly during the First World War. Pierre Réjon, born on Martinique, served in the French Air Force during the First World War. Domenico Mondelli, a Tigrayan, served in the Italian Air Force during the conflict, while Ahmet Ali Çelikten fought for the Ottoman empire. On the British side, William Robinson Clarke, a Jamaican, served initially as a mechanic and later as a pilot in the Royal Flying Corps. He was wounded in July 1917 while on a photographic mission, as he later described in a letter to his mother:

> I was doing some photographs a few miles the other side when about five Hun scouts came down upon me, and before I could get away, I got a bullet through the spine. I managed to pilot the machine nearly back to the aerodrome, but had to put her down as I was too weak to fly any more … My observer escaped without any injury.[3]

After recovering from his injuries, he was declared unfit for flying and continued to serve as a mechanic.

After the First World War, the opportunities for Black Americans that wanted to fly remained limited. It motivated them to look for other possibilities. Bessie Coleman, a woman of African-American and Native American descent, was determined to fly and she eventually made her way to France, where she acquired her pilot's license in 1921 before returning to America to give airshows. A paying audience of Black and white Americans alike could watch her perform tricks and acrobatics in the air; tragically, on 30 April 1926 during a flight in preparation for a parachute jump, her aircraft suddenly went into a dive and she fell from the plane. Coleman was dead on impact, while her mechanic, William D. Wills, perished when the plane struck the ground.

Although the United States of America claimed to fight for democracy during the Second World War, it was far from an equal society.

Within the same country, "separate, but equal" societies existed for white, Black and Asian Americans, enforced to a stricter or less strict degree, depending on the local circumstances. Racism and discrimination were common, especially in the Southern States. Restaurants, schools, even toilets could be segregated. Although the idea of the "separate but equal" doctrine was that there would be separate facilities for the different races, it often resulted in inferior facilities for Black Americans.

The basis for the "separate but equal" doctrine was provided by the US Supreme Court's decision in the case of Plessy vs Ferguson in 1896. In 1892, Homer Plessy, a man of mixed descent, boarded a whites-only train. In doing so, Plessy violated Louisiana's Separate Car Act of 1890, which claimed to provide equal but separate facilities for white and non-white passengers. The case escalated up to the US Supreme Court, which ruled that the Louisiana law did not violate the Fourteenth Amendment of the US Constitution. It provided the legal basis for several segregation laws, which marked the difference between white and Black Americans. The laws separating the Americans based upon race became infamously known as the Jim Crow laws.

In the case of Black Americans, they were often portrayed in a stereotypical way, referred to as "Jim Crow", originally a stage character in the 1830s and 1840s performed by the white entertainer Thomas Dartmouth Rice. The performance gave a racist portrayal of Black American people and their culture. With the passage of time this racist character's name, "Jim Crow", was used to encompass the segregation system in southern American states, where the Black Americans were denied equal rights as Americans and relegated to second-class citizens. Just like the caricature's portrayal, which was a misrepresentation of Black American culture, the law was used to misrepresent Black Americans, thus being known as "Jim Crow laws".

Transgressions of the segregation system were harshly punished. One of the worst possible outcomes was lynching, where someone was killed without a fair trail. These violent acts were committed in public by a lawless mob, usually by white Americans against Black Americans, based upon real or perceived crimes. The NAACP estimates 4,743 lynchings between 1882 and 1968.

Racial prejudice was common during the 1930s and 1940s, and many white Americans considered themselves superior to Black Americans. Around 120,000 Japanese Americans were incarcerated in special camps shortly after the attack on Pearl Harbor, because the American government mistrusted the loyalties of these people after what became known as the "Niihau incident", where a captured Japanese pilot was assisted in his escape by two Japanese Americans. The pilot was eventually killed in a struggle with a native islander, while the Japanese American killed himself. The tensions rose further when Japanese Americans were suspected of spying for the Japanese government and passing along information.

Black American Soldiers

Despite being a segregated society, Black Americans were in combat from the first day of America entering the Second World War. When Pearl Harbor was suddenly attacked early in the morning of 7 December 1941 by the Imperial Japanese Navy, mess attendant second class Doris Miller assisted wounded sailors and manned an anti-aircraft gun, firing at the Japanese planes. Initially he was not credited for his actions. Only after much pressure from the Black press was Miller's name published and did he receive public recognition, being awarded the Navy Cross. Miller died on 24 November 1943, when the ship he served on was struck by enemy torpedo's and sank. His body was never recovered.

In spite of Miller's action, and the heroism of Black Americans, the general belief was that Black Americans were unfit for combat and so their service was largely relegated to support units. The exceptions were the segregated combat units that existed. Three tank battalions, the 761st, the 758th, and the 784th Tank Battalion fought in battle. Three tank destroyer battalions, the 614th, 679th, and the 827th Tank Destroyer Battalion, served in combat. The 333rd, 578th, 686th, 777th, and the 999th Field Artillery Battalion provided artillery support for the units to which they were attached. Third Platoon, C Company, of the 614th Tank Destroyer Battalion was the first segregated unit to win the Distinguished Unit Citation for engaging the enemy at Climbach, France. The 969th Field Artillery Battalion was surrounded at Bastogne in December 1944 and would fight alongside the 101st Airborne Division. Finally, it would earn the Distinguished Unit Citation, becoming the second segregated unit to do so.

While the 92nd Infantry Division fought in Italy, the 93rd Infantry Division was employed in the Pacific. The 555th Parachute Infantry Battalion, an all-Black airborne unit, did not fight overseas, but instead combatted forest fires in the US caused by Japanese Fu-Go balloon bombs. These floating bombs were used against the United States and were intended to spread panic. Although the uncontrolled bombs were released into the air and allowed to float all the way to North America, they failed to reach the aspired result. Meanwhile, anti-aircraft battalions, such as the 452nd and the 870th Anti-Aircraft Artillery Battalion watched the skies and protected against hostile aircraft. Black women also served, for example in the 6888th Central Postal Directory Battalion, which sorted mail for soldiers in Europe.

Although there were Black units serving in combat, other segregated combat units were never employed for their intended task. The 846th and 795th Tank Destroyer Battalion were the earliest two segregated tank destroyer units established, but both were disbanded and their soldiers sent to other units. The 9th Cavalry Regiment and the 10th Cavalry Regiment both reached North Africa, before they, too, were disbanded and provided soldiers for other units.

The opportunities for Black Americans to serve were still far fewer than those for white Americans. However, there were around 12.8 million Black people in America, amounting to 9.8 per cent of the total population of the United States – a significant pool of potential recruits that could not be neglected.

The army failed to fully exploit this potential manpower because, shockingly, they were still guided by a 1925 study entitled: "Employment of Negro Man Power in War", which was to "be accepted as the War Department policy" in handling recruitment "until a more complete study be made on the subject by the General staff".[4]

The report contained a multitude of racist attitudes, one of which was:

> [The Black] can not control himself in the fear of danger to the extent the white man can. He has not the initiative and resourcefulness of the white man. He is mentally inferior to the white man.[5]

The notes for a proposed plan included the assertion that:

> the Negro does not perform his share of civil duties in time of peace in proportion to his population. He has no leaders in industrial or commercial life. He takes no part in government. Compared to the white man he is admittedly of inferior mentality. He is inherently weaker in character.[6]

Likewise, the War College formed the following opinion:

> In the process of evolution the American Negro has not progressed as far as the other sub-species of the human family. As a race he has not developed leadership qualities. His mental inferiority and the inherent weaknesses of his character are factors that must be considered with great care in the preparation of any plan for his employment in war.

By any standards these attitudes are shocking, but they set the tone for the decades to come and hampered the US Armed Forces in their development. Black Americans were unjustly viewed as "inferior", their talents were wasted and they were denied equal opportunities both in the military service as well as in life. Furthermore, the systemic and societal racism meant resources were wasted in maintaining a segregated system; two facilities needed to be present, rather than the same one being used by both Black and white Americans.

The *Luftwaffe*

While America had planned to remain neutral in any European conflict, Germany had anticipated for several years what was to become the Second World War. The independent Luftwaffe was established in March 1935, although in the previous few years Germany had built up its forces in secret under the cover of the German Air Sports Association. Hermann Göring was the first Air Minister of the newly formed *Luftwaffe*, which had its first taste of combat when the Condor Legion participated in the Spanish Civil War (1936–39).

Although the organization would be influenced by local conditions, in general, the *Geschwader* consisted of a staff unit and three or four *Gruppen.* These groups contained three to four squadrons, called *staffeln,* of ten to twelve aircraft. Each *Geschwader* thus contained between 90 and 120 aircraft.

Initially, at the start of beginning of hostilities with France and England in 1939, the Luftwaffe was well equipped and highly trained. It excelled in close-support for ground troops and used dive-bombers to clear a path for the blitzkrieg, allowing ground elements to proceed rapidly. As a result of this strategy though, the Luftwaffe had few long-range bombers.

During the Battle of Britain, fought from July to October 1940, the German air force attempted to destroy the British Royal Air Force and soften up the British defenses for a potential invasion. The Luftwaffe was incapable of keeping up with the attrition rates and failed to replace valuable losses in bombers and fighters, losing 1,977 aircraft between 10 July and 30 October, while the RAF lost 1,744 aircraft.

Furthermore, from 22 June 1941 the Eastern Front was opened up when the Axis declared war on the Soviet Union, and involved a front all the way from Finland in the north to Ukraine in the south. Compared with the battles fought on the eastern frontiers of Europe, and the defense of the Third Reich against Allied bombers, the German air force in the Mediterranean was considered of lesser importance. In 1943 the Allied fighters established air superiority in the Mediterranean theater and the Luftwaffe was short of aircraft.[7] The role of German fighters diminished steadily, especially as more units were pulled out of Italy after the Normandy landings in France on D-Day in the summer of 1944, or were employed in the defence of Germany against the Allied bombing campaign.

The two main fighters of the Luftwaffe were the Messerschmitt Bf 109 and the Focke-Wulf 190. The Me-109, or Bf 109 as it was known to German pilots, had its first flight in May 1935. It was used during the Spanish Civil War and in the beginning of the Second World War. The plane received several improvements throughout the war, but by the war's end was outclassed by the American P-51 Mustang.

The Focke-Wulf first flew in June 1939. It was superior to the then common version of the British Spitfire. However, the FW-190 had a limited operational history and had a slower top speed than the P-51. For example, the FW-190 A-8 had a maximum speed of 652 km/h (405 mph) compared to the 710 km/h (440 mph) of a P-51D.

The Experiment

Americans of all races were interested in airplanes, but it was difficult for Black people who wished to join the Army Air Corps. There were segregated units in the cavalry, and there were specialized infantry regiments where Black Americans could serve, but there existed no such segregated units in the American Army Air Corps. Cadet Benjamin O. Davis, who would later command the 332nd Fighter Group, was rejected by the Army Air Corps in 1935. There was simply no Black unit to which he could be assigned.

Despite difficulties, some Black Americans managed to acquire military experience. Two such pilots were James Peck and John Robinson. James Peck flew in the Spanish Republican Air Force during the Spanish Civil War. He was initially turned down by the US Air Corps and went to Spain in 1936, joining the Republican Air Force. Upon his return from his service, he was rejected by the US armed forces and found work as a civilian. John Robinson served as the commander of the Ethiopian Air Force during the Second Italo-Ethiopian War in 1935 and 1936, becoming finally known as the "Brown Condor" of Ethiopia. Interviewed shortly before the outbreak of hostilities, Robinson shared his thoughts on the war:

> For some days I have been doing patrol duty over the Eritrean front and then I returned here and patrolled the eastern part of Ethiopia which is along the frontier of Italian Somaliland. We are using a 550 horsepower French airplane, which frankly, I don't like, but the chief of the aviation corps is a Frenchman, most of the planes are French.
>
> If war actually starts and the Italians plan to use their vaunted air escadrille, they are in for more difficulties than any land fighter or layman, so to speak, can understand. I have flown in the heights in the United States, but in flying here, have suffered a little from "air sickness". Now I feel used to it, but it is very seldom that a pilot has to fly over 6,000ft high and to do any successful bombing from such an altitude, one has about one chance out of six thousand to do any damage to the particular target he was aiming for.[8]

Robinson concluded that the Italian airplanes would be more of a psychological threat than a physical threat. Despite Robinson's thinking, by the time the article appeared in the US newspapers on 5 October 1935, the invasion had already been underway for forty-eight hours. The war ended in May 1936 with the annexation of Ethiopia by Italy.

In that year, Robinson returned to the United States, where he received recognition for his actions in Ethiopia.

In May 1939 two other Black Americans, Dale White and Chauncey Spencer, attempted the Goodwill Flight, flying from Chicago to Washington, D.C. Both men had experienced great difficulty in pursuing their dreams of aviation due to their race, but managed to overcome this with the help of others. It was in Chicago, Illinois, that they could complete their flight training and in an act of daring, together with the support of the Black press, they would prove that Black Americans were capable of flying.

White was chosen as the pilot and Spencer was selected as the navigator, flying in a rented Lincoln-Page PT-K. This was an open-cockpit two-seat biplane aircraft, made of welded steel, for the fuselage, and spruce bars and basswood ribs for the wings. They made the flight because it had been impossible for Black Americans to join the US Army Air Corps and they wished to change this. The pair completed the trip, despite mechanical difficulties along the way, and landed safely in Washington, D.C.

Once there the two men met various senators, including Harry S. Truman, who was interested in their endeavor and reportedly said: "If you guys had the guts to fly this thing to Washington, I've got the guts enough to see you get what you're asking."

From the mid-1930s the European nations started training civilian pilots as a way of building up their air forces. The United States began a similar program in 1938 – the Civilian Pilot Training Program (CPTP). The idea was to create a pool of pilots that could be employed for military purposes in times of war. Truman helped pass legislation that allowed Black Americans to participate in the Program.

Women also became pilots, and many female flyers served as Women's Airforce Service Pilots (WASP), and would ferry planes to their destination. As Harry Stewart, a pilot in the 332nd Fighter Group, would encounter during his training when he came upon another P-47 Thunderbolt and got into a mock dogfight. After being bested, he discovered that the pilot had been a woman.

Although initially African Americans could not participate in the program, pressure mounted on Congress to open it for all Americans; Congress passed the Civilian Pilot Training Act on 27 June 1939, which included a provision that no one was excluded based upon race. Funding was secured for extending the CPTP program to a few Black universities: Howard University, Hampton Institute, North Carolina A&T, West Virginia State, and Delaware State. Later, on 15 October 1939, the Tuskegee Institute in Alabama would be added to this list. Alongside the pilots, ground units were trained to facilitate the planes and personnel. Black people now had the chance to learn to fly and to share in the burden of defending the United States when necessary.

Tuskegee Institute was a Black college founded in 1881 by Booker T. Washington, and Tuskegee Army Air Field served as the most prominent training location for Black American soldiers. The ground crew trained at Chanute Army Air Field, Illinois, although later they were also trained at Tuskegee. The construction of Moton Field, in the vicinity of Tuskegee, started in June 1941. Initially, training was in Stearman PT-17. This biplane was the primary trainer of the United States Army Air Corps during the Second World War. Later the pilots moved on to Vultee BT-13, a mono-wing plane. This plane was nicknamed the 'Vibrator', for which there are several possible explanations. It could be that the canopy started rattling or that the plane started shuddering when approaching a stall, or that the radial engine and the fixed-pitch propeller caused all the windows on the base to vibrate whenever a BT-13 took off. Lastly, training moved on to the AT-6 Texans.

President Roosevelt, during the 1940 campaign for the presidency, courted Black voters and issued a statement on 9 October 1940 that Black Americans would serve in proportionate numbers in combat and non-combat roles. This included aviation.

The flight program at Tuskegee received another boost when the First Lady Eleanor Roosevelt got into a plane with Charles Alfred "Chief" Anderson. Although her bodyguards warned against it, she boarded the Piper J-3 Cub and went up in the air. A picture was snapped after their return and it gave much publicity to the program. It showed the world that Black pilots could fly as well as white, gave exposure to the program, and made it clear they had the support and trust of the First Lady.

The situation at Tuskegee was not perfect, since the nearest airport in Montgomery was around 40 miles [65 kilometers] away. A small airport was created at Tuskegee, where three Piper Cubs could take off and the students did not have to travel such a distance every time.

A secondary program followed for more complex training. Pilots could be trained for single-engine aircraft, as well as pilots for twin-engine aircraft and liaison pilots. Liaison pilots performed a variety of vital tasks, although not as glamorous as the fighter pilots. Liaisons performed reconnaissance, but also the delivery of supplies to the front lines and medical evacuations. In addition to pilots, mechanics and support staff were also trained.

In November 1941, the first commander of Tuskegee Army Airfield, TAAF, arrived: Major James Ellison, although he was transferred following an incident in the town of Tuskegee. A Black military policeman wanted to take custody of a Black soldier who had been arrested and was in the town jail. A disagreement with the town's law enforcement ensued, with the military policeman and his driver arrested in the escalating situation. Major Ellison became involved and got them released. The white residents of Tuskegee took offence to this and not long after, in January 1942, Ellison was relieved by Colonel Frederick von Kimble. Kimble was a controversial commander, cooperating

An engine mechanic reveals the hidden mysteries of a P-40 engine to a class in Allison liquid-cooled motors. Aviation cadets studying together with members of the field's enlisted personnel, Tuskegee Army Air Field, Alabama. (Courtesy of Library of Congress)

Fuel system being explained to Black aircraft mechanics. (Courtesy of Library of Congress)

Students are being taught how to send and receive code. (Courtesy of National Archives and Records Administration)

with curfew laws against Black soldiers and refused to promote Black Americans above the rank of captain, while also allowing Black military police to be harassed by white local police officers. These and other incidents were written about in the Black press and eventually von Kimble was replaced by Colonel Noel Parrish, on 26 December 1942.

Although Parrish could not eliminate segregation entirely on the base, he did show devotion to his men. Noel Parrish was the white commander that ensured the experiment succeeded. Through his fair treatment, the Black soldiers benefited.

The 99th Pursuit Squadron

In October 1940 Benjamin O. Davis, Sr. was promoted to brigadier general, becoming the first Black American to hold that rank. In December that year, the Army Air Corps came up with the plan to establish a Black pursuit squadron. On 22 March 1941 the 99th Pursuit Squadron was established – the first segregated squadron. It was redesignated as the 99th Fighter Squadron on 15 May 1942.

On 19 July 1941 the first class was inducted and out of the twelve men, five graduated on 7 March 1942: Captain Benjamin O. Davis Jr., and second lieutenants Lemuel R. Custis, Charles DeBow, George S. Roberts, Mac Ross. They were joined on 29 April 1942 by the second lieutenants: Sidney P. Brooks, Charles W. Dryden, Clarence C. Jamison. New classes joined them every month.

A major force in the establishment was Benjamin O. Davis Jr., the son of Davis Sr., the brigadier general. As the son of an officer, Davis Jr. was destined to follow in his father's footsteps. When the younger Davis enrolled in the US Military Academy at West Point, he had to endure four years of silencing. As he described it:

> just when I thought that I was getting along extremely well—that life at West Point, even for plebes, was a piece of cake—the roof fell in. I was in my room shining my shoes and brass when I heard a knock on the door announcing a meeting in the sinks (the basement) in 10 minutes. As I approached the assembly where the meeting was in

Army Air Corps cadets reporting to Captain Benjamin O. Davis, Jr. (Courtesy of National Archives and Records Administration)

progress, I heard someone ask, "What are we going to do about the nigger?" I realized then that the meeting was about me, and I was not supposed to attend. I turned on my heel and double-timed back to my room.

From that meeting on, the cadets who roomed across the hall, who had been friendly earlier, no longer spoke to me. In fact, no one spoke to me except in the line of duty. Apparently, certain upper-class cadets had determined that I was getting along too well at the Academy to suit them, and they were going to enforce an old West Point tradition—"silencing"—with the object of making my life so unhappy that I would resign. Silencing had been applied in the past to certain cadets who were considered to have violated the honor code and refused to resign. In my case there was no question of such a violation, which would have been formally cited by the Honor Committee; I was to be silenced solely because cadets did not want blacks at West Point. Their only purpose was to freeze me out. What they did not realize was that I was stubborn enough to put up with their treatment to reach the goal I had come to attain.[9]

Despite the silencing, Davis used this a motivation to go on. He was determined to succeed and explained how he managed all those years:

> This cruel treatment was designed to make me buckle, but I refused to buckle in any way. I maintained my self-respect. First, I did not mention my troubles in letters to my mother and father. Second, I made my mind up that I would continue to hold my head high. At no time did I consciously show that I was hurt; even at this early date, I took solace in the fact that I was mature enough to live through anything other people might submit me to, particularly people I considered to be misguided. I kept telling myself that I was superior in character to them, even to the point of feeling sorry for them. Certainly, I was not missing anything by not associating with them; instead, I bolstered my feelings by thinking that they were missing a great deal by not knowing me.[10]

In October 1935, when approaching graduation, Davis applied for the Army Air Corps. As mentioned earlier, he was rejected because there were no segregated units to which he could be assigned. Years later, when the army did make serious plans to establish a Black squadron, he

Officer returns salute as he passes the cadets lined up during review. (Courtesy of National Archives and Records Administration)

Captain Benjamin O. Davis Jr. climbing into an Advanced Trainer. (Courtesy of National Archives and Records Administration)

was an obvious choice for leading it. Although Davis was not a natural pilot, he was a good leader and he used his leadership skills to tangle with the Germans and Jim Crow in the fights to come.

As with all armies during wars, accidents happened both during training and in the field. In this case, where accidents involved fast machines and steel, there was a high risk of fatalities and or serious injuries. On 8 June 1942, cadet Richard Dawson died in an accident. It would be the first loss of life. As Dryden described it:

> Two cadets in the advanced phase were flying an AT-6 on a routine training mission when they attempted to fly under a bridge across the Tallapoosa River west of the base. Somehow, they didn't make it. The plane crashed and broke in half between the front and rear cockpits. Cadet Richard "Red" Dawson, in the front seat, was killed instantly. Cadet Walter I. Lawson was found sitting on the bank of the river, dazed and bruised, but alive. Miraculously, surprisingly alive![11]

Lawson would be known as "Ghost" afterwards.

On 12 September 1942, Faythe McGinnis became the first of the graduated Tuskegee Airmen to die. He was set to be married the next day.[12] On 30 January 1943, Richard C. Davis was killed when his P-40 crashed. Earl King was killed in a crash on 24 March 1943. More casualties, both at home and on the front, were to follow.

On 26 May 1942, another segregated squadron, the 100th Fighter Squadron, was activated. The 99th Fighter Squadron was no longer alone. Charles DeBow and Mac Ross were assigned to this new squadron. On 13 October 1942, the 301st Fighter Squadron and the 302nd Fighter Squadron were activated. These squadrons formed part of the 332nd Fighter Group, which was activated on the same day and consisted of the 100th Fighter Squadron, as well as the two previously mentioned units.

The 99th FS had not received orders yet and people were wondering if the unit would ever be employed in combat. On 20 February, almost two years after its activation, the question remained unanswered. As appeared in the *Pittsburgh Courier*:

> Hanging over the whole scene is one big question. When is the 99th going to move? Its pilots have over two hundred hours in the air, although the number piled up by white fighter pilots before going to a combat zone is not usually more than forty. The 99th have been on the alert for the last six months. They can have no leave to go home. The enlisted men cannot be freed to go to OCS. Everyone is jumpy; nerves are on edge. A squadron fights in a group of three. No one can predict whether the 99th will be sent out with white squadrons or will have to wait until the 100th and the 301st are ready. A fighter group escorts a bomber and the War Department has announced that no Negroes are going to be permitted to fly bombers. Will it permit Negro fighter pilots to escort a white bomber squadron? Probably there are plenty who would be glad to have with them these competent young men.[13]

On 1 April 1943, the 99th Fighter Squadron finally received orders to go overseas. On 15 April 1943 the squadron embarked on the troopship

Mariposa and left the United States behind. On 24 April 1943, the *Mariposa* arrived at its destination – Casablanca, Morocco.

One of the men, Louis Purnell, had a bottle of Coca-Cola and decided it would be saved as a prize for the first man in the unit to score an aerial kill. Until that time, it was kept in the squadron safe.

The squadron finally got orders to move to a new base at Oued Nja, near Fez, arriving there on 29 April.

"DESTINATION BERLIN!!"

A propaganda cartoon about the 99th Fighter Squadron. (Courtesy of National Archives and Records Administration)

Chapter 2

Service in Africa and Sicily

First contact with the enemy

In North Africa, the 99th moved to Oued Nja, near the city Fez, and arrived at a former Luftwaffe base. The place was littered with derelict aircraft. Wrecked Me-109s were all around them. The squadron waited for a week before their aircraft arrived, but then they finally received twenty-seven Curtiss P-40Ls.

The Curtiss P-40 Warhawk was a fighter and ground-attack aircraft, also employed by the British and Soviet Air Forces. Derived from the P-36, it could be produced rapidly. The first test fight had been in 1938 and the fighter continued to serve until the end of the Second World War.

While the men were at Oud Nja, they were assisted by three white pilots. They were Philip Cochran, Major Ralph Keyes and Major Robert Fackler. These experienced pilots stayed a week and provided advice. As Dryden recalled:

> we still lacked a vital ingredient, however: combat-wise veterans among our leaders. The next best thing was to be tutored by combat veterans. Soon after we got our planes, we were visited by one of the best fighter pilots in the business at that time: Colonel Philip Cochran, the real-life model for the Colonel "Flip Corkin" of the popular "Terry and the Pirates" cartoon. During the Allies' desert campaign against Field Marshal Erwin Rommel's Afrika Corps, Colonel Cochran had proved his dive-bombing skill by dropping a 500-pounder smack atop a Nazi high command headquarters. He had also developed dogfighting tactics

in several skirmishes with Luftwaffe pilots. Along with two other P-40 combat veterans of the desert campaign, Major Ralph Keyes and Major Robert Fackler, he spent about a week with us at Oued Nja. We learned much about our adversaries from that trio. For me the most important information was about how our P-40L "Kittyhawks" compared with Field Marshal Hermann Goering's fleet of fighters. Colonel Cochran told us that because both of the primary fighter planes being used by the Luftwaffe in the theater of operations, the Me-109 and the FW-190, could outrun, outclimb, and outdive the P-40, we were going to be among the most courageous pilots in the war. We would have to stay and fight simply because we were too slow to be able to run away!

"Don't worry about that, however," he told us, "Because the P-40 can outturn every fighter the Germans have except one built by the Italians, the Macchi 202. But there are not many of those in the theater. So, all you have to do when you get jumped by an Me-109 or a Focke Wulf is to get into a tight turn, reef it in as tight as you can without stalling, and just wait him out. If he tries to stay with you in the turn, you will eventually end up on his tail."

With such information, and many other tidbits of tactics and techniques of survival in aerial combat, I felt more than ever ready for my baptism of fire.[1]

Mishaps and accidents were still a risk. While at the base, Bud Clark's landing gear refused to be lowered. To avoid the additional risks of landing with excess fuel, he circled in the air until all the fuel had been used up and then attempted to land on the belly with minimal damage. Leon Roberts clipped a cable and lost part of his rudder and vertical stabilizer, but still managed to get the airplane safely back.

In the end of May 1943, the men moved to Fardjouna. As the squadron history recounted after their departure from Oued Nja:

On 30 May 1943, at approximately 13:30 hours, a group of pilots of the 99th Fighter Squadron took off in P-40s for their new landing field. There was an air echelon for mechanics, and enough supplies with which to operate until the ground echelon arrived.

The first section of the ground echelon left Oued Nja by boxcars on the same day. Three days later, the motor convoy departed from the camp at Oued Nja. Both ground echelons arrived 7 June, 1943, at Fardjouna landing ground.[2]

About Fardjouna, Charles Dryden recalled:

In their headlong rush to escape advancing Allied armies, the Germans left a lot of equipment in the vicinity of our airstrip. Some of our men claimed ownership of abandoned vehicles: J.B. Knighten had found a German jeep; Gene Carter had a motorcycle. Here and there one could see the hulks of crashed airplanes, both Allied and German, that were great sources of souvenirs. The main problem with scrounging mementos from German equipment was the risk of being booby-trapped and suffering injury or death. The only souvenir I got up enough nerve to take was the clock from the instrument panel of a wrecked British Spitfire.

Booby traps could be found out in the fields around Fardjouna. The most common ones were the Italian-made "tomatoes," red hand-grenades that were left behind by fleeing Nazis who had sown the surrounding area with a number of the lethal "fruit." The local Arab men avoided the danger of the "tomatoes" by riding their spindly legged donkeys while their wives walked ahead. One day an Arab woman came to our dispensary to ask our medics for help. Her hand had just been blown off by a booby trap. That's all I needed to convince me that the only souvenir I wanted to take home from the war was me, intact, uninjured.[3]

The squadron was attached to the 33rd Fighter Group, of the Twelfth Air Force, under the command of Colonel William "Spike" Momyer.

The 33rd Fighter Group, consisting of seventy-seven fighters, had suffered serious losses on 10 November 1942, when a pilot and his aircraft disappeared in the fog, another plane splashed into the sea after taking off from the escort carrier USS Chenango (CVE-28), and seventeen more planes were wrecked upon their first landing in the theater.[4] To make up the losses, the 99th Fighter Squadron was assigned to the unit.

There was little love between the two units from the start. When Davis and Roberts reported and saluted, Momyer did not salute back; he was both ignorant and offensive. On 3 June he moved the time of a briefing forward by an hour so that the 99th men arrived late.

Pilots of the 99th FS would fly in support of the 33rd FG. William Campbell, who had a brother serving with the 614th Tank Destroyer Battalion, and Clarence Jamison both took part in a mission with the 33rd Fighter Group as pilots. Several hours later another detachment involved James Wiley and Charles B. Hall. The objective was the German-held airfield on the Italian island of Pantelleria, to bomb and strafe it. Momyer had selected Wiley as his wingman. All planes carried 500-lb bombs.

The next day, Dryden experienced his first combat engagement:

> Midafternoon, June 4, I saw shots fired at me in anger, with malice aforethought and with intent to kill! And certainly, with provocation because, in a screaming dive, the way Colonel Cochran had taught us to do when we were just learning back at Oued Nja, I was attempting to place a 500-pound bomb on a German target on Pantelleria. Following my leader in the dive I saw red tracers streaking past my cockpit, hundreds of them looking like a river of red sparkles that I saw out of the corners of my eyes and not directly because I was focused on the gunsight mounted atop the instrument panel. Concentrating on hitting the target, I didn't have time to get scared. It wasn't until I pulled up from the bomb run that the thought crossed my mind: "They were trying to kill me!" Only then did I tweak a bit.[5]

Being fired upon by a hostile ground target is different than an encounter with enemy aircraft, which happened a few days later on 9 June, when the pilots provided cover for several A-20 bombers. Spann Watson fired from a long distance and the Germans abandoned the fight. As Charles Dryden recalled:

> Up until that very moment I had harbored a fear deep within myself. It wasn't as much a fear of the enemy as it was the fear of which President Franklin Roosevelt spoke when he proclaimed that "the only thing we have to fear is fear itself." When I saw the swastikas on those Me-109s and felt the urge to "go get 'em" and a surge of adrenaline at the prospect of being the first Negro to shoot down an enemy airplane in aerial combat, I knew that I had conquered my fear of possibly turning yellow and turning tail at the first sign of the enemy.
>
> As it turned out none of us scored a victory on that mission. Ashley damaged one of the enemy planes but wasn't able to follow the smoking plane to see if it crashed, and we did not have gun cameras at that stage of the war so he could not confirm a victory.[6]

Although the men were excited about their first encounter with the enemy, Momyer would base his negative opinion on the early exchanges of the 99th Fighter Squadron with the enemy, claiming that the pilots lacked aggressiveness and that the formations would disintegrate under fire.

The pilots came through the Pantellerian campaign without a mishap; it ended on 11 June 1943 when the island surrendered. It would become the first territory that surrendered by the use of solely airpower. The 33rd moved to El Haouaria to prepare for combat in Sicily. The 99th Fighter Squadron was briefly attached to the 324th Fighter Group, from the end of June until the middle of July, before returning to the 33rd Fighter Group.

On 2 July, the unit was assigned as escort to sixteen bombers that would attack the German airfield in Castelvetrano. The first bomber missed the starting point for its run and the other planes circled above the target. The German fighters scrambled to meet them in the air. The B-25s finally dropped their bombs and climbed into the air to return to Africa. The Germans, meanwhile, descended on them. Sherman White and

Black pilots in one of the flight formations which will soon carry them over enemy territory. (Courtesy of National Archives and Records Administration)

Captain Charles B. Hall was the first member of the 99th Fighter Squadron to shoot down an enemy fighter. He shot down two more on 28 January 1944. (Courtesy of National Archives and Records Administration)

James McCullen were lost. Charles Hall spotted 2 Focke-Wulfs trailing the bombers and positioned himself behind one of them. He fired a long burst into it and it became the first aerial victory of the day.

As Charles Hall later explained:

> It was my eighth mission, but the first time I had seen the enemy close enough to shoot at him. I saw two Focke-Wulfs following the Mitchells just after the bombs were dropped. I headed for the space between the fighters and bombers and managed to turn inside the Jerries. I fired a long burst and saw my traces penetrate the second aircraft. He was turning to the left, but suddenly fell off and headed straight into the ground. I followed him down and saw him crash. He raised a big cloud of dust.[7]

For Charles Dryden this mission symbolized something different. As he recalled about this experience:

> Airplane accidents have a sobering effect on aviators, reminding them that they themselves are also vulnerable to the forces of nature, machine malfunctions, or their own pilot error. Our first encounters with the death of comrades were rough enough. Our baptism by fire, in the sky over Sicily, was even more so. More so because it was different. Different because in Sicily our mates were shot down by guns fired in anger. With malice aforethought and intent to kill. Of course, our ground school training as aviation cadets had included viewing the War Department training film, Kill or Be Killed. It succeeded in convincing us that in war "it's them or us." Add to that my outrage over Nazi atrocities, generally, plus arrogant Aryan claims of racial superiority, particularly, and I was well motivated to fight Hitler and his gangsters. And to lay my life on the line for my country, if need be.[8]

Upon his return, Hall did a victory roll and he got to enjoy the bottle of Coca-Cola that had been kept for this purpose. In the afternoon, General Eisenhower visited the 99th Fighter Squadron to congratulate the unit on its first victory and to inspire them for more great deeds. Eisenhower was accompanied by James H. Doolittle, Carl Spaatz, and John Cannon.

However, not all pilots experienced victories and many had frightening encounters on similar missions. As Allen Lane explained:

> I had a chilling experience when Germans attacked the squadron last June while it was escorting British bombers over Sicily. I was teamed up with lieutenant Herbert Allen Clark […]. Two Me-109s picked us out. Clark and I turned to meet them. We were darned busy for a while, shooting and getting shot at. Meanwhile, although too busy to see, I had a feeling Clark and I were drifting apart. My suspicion was confirmed during a breath-taking spell when I didn't see a single friend, only my persistent German who was coming again. His plane was awful fast. I turned to meet the attack, pressing the gun button in the meantime. The guns didn't respond. I realized then that the ammunition was exhausted. While the German climbed and turned for another attack, I dived to get away, starting at about 10,000ft. The movement caught the German flatfooted. At 3,500ft, I began emerging, diving finally. I leveled out at 1,000ft, looked around and that darned German had dived too, leveling off behind me. Two minutes later, he attacked again and I turned into him again, bluffing him away. He was afraid of my guns, not knowing they were not loaded. This happened two more times until, almost nearing the coast of North Africa, I spied my squadron ahead and Capt. Charles B. Hall of Brazil, Ind., and Lt. William Campbell of Tuskegee Institute, Ala., looked back and came to my rescue. Until then, I sure thought I would wake up and find my goose cooked.[9]

Walter, "Ghost" Lawson, had a similar experience:

> A mean flock of Me-109s appeared above. One very bold German dived, trying to get through my position to attack the bombers. I shot him, apparently damaging the plane which spiraled downward. I took my eyes off the falling

plane in the nick of time. I looked to the rear and another German was diving almost on top of me. I had just time to nose around toward him. We passed each other like rockets. Some instinct made me look downward in the opposite direction and I saw another Messerschmitt coming upward in puffs of smoke. Its cannon indicated that the German was shooting at me. I wheeled, nosed downward into him and fired my guns. I saw bullets spatter on the German's fuselage. He went into a tailspin. I looked around and saw I was friendless with ten more Germans flying in formation close to the ground, but they apparently didn't see me. I decided to get close to the ground and run home. I was about 20 miles inland. As I left Sicily behind me, I saw the tails of two planes sticking out in the Mediterranean Sea and I recognized one as an Me-109. I believe I bagged two German planes that day, but I am unable to make a claim, because I was too busy following them downward to witness the crash.[10]

The Allied forces were preparing for the invasion of Sicily and it included a lot of bombarding.

Spann Watson, of Hackensack N.J., recounted such an experience:

Hell broke loose one July afternoon when the squadron was serving as medium cover for American bombers over Sicily. A white squadron above was serving as top cover and became engaged in a dogfight with about a score of Germans. I couldn't afford to spend too much time looking, but with a quick glance I saw groups of planes swishing in and out of clouds, spiraling, climbing, and circling like a great circus. Meanwhile, the bombers were drawing away. Suddenly something happened to my plane; I checked quickly and discovered the radio and power system were out of commission and the guns were not working. The propeller rose too high, overheating the motor. To prevent burning up, I reduced my speed to about 125 miles an hour and dropped from 10,000ft to 6,000ft. I decided to bail out as soon as I reached the Mediterranean, but when I got there the plane was holding its own, although it was awfully slow. I saw Me-109s several times and my heart jumped, but they didn't see me. The trip home seemed the longest plane flight I ever made.[11]

On 6 July, Marshal Coningham of the RAF visited the squadron and explained the British operational procedures, and on 9 July the Allies invaded Sicily. The Tuskegee Airmen flew cover over the Sicilian skies to stop the Luftwaffe from harassing the invaders. On 11 July, Lieutenant Dick Bolling was shot down by anti-aircraft fire from ships off the coast of Licata. The squadron history noted:

> Lieutenant Bolling bailed out and was seen by First Lieutenant William Campbell to get into a dinghy. His position was radioed in by Lieutenant Campbell. When Lieutenant Bolling returned to camp on 15 July, he stated that he remained in the dinghy approximately twenty-four hours before being picked up by an Allied destroyer. He was greatly dismayed to see many naval vessels passing by in the distance. Finally despairing of being rescued, the lieutenant attracted the destroyer by standing up in the dinghy and waving part of his parachute which he had tied to the dinghy.[12]

He arrived in time to travel with the unit to its new location. On 19 July 29 C-47s departed from Fardjouna, carrying supplies and personnel to their new station: Sicily. The ground echelon remained to finish wrapping up and prepared to travel by sea to their new station.

The unit would not take part in combat missions, being used for ground support instead. On 25 July the first replacements arrived: Lieutenants Baugh, Toppins, and Morgan. On 27 July, Major General House visited the squadron. On the same day, Technical Sergeant Edsel Jett, a member of the ground echelon, drowned after being caught in the undertow offshore. He swam out to rescue another drowning soldier, but lost his own life in doing so.

On 11 August Graham Mitchell died, as described by Samuel M. Bruce:

> I collided with another plane in mid-air at an altitude of 1,500ft. The squadron was just starting a mission and our planes were just getting into formation. [...] I was assigned to a place between planes and was just getting positioned when another plane, far to my right, developed engine trouble, lost height, and veered left into my path. A collision seemed unavoidable, but I nosed upward for a split second and I thought we missed, but, with a lighting crunch, my propeller chopped the tail off the other plane flown by Lieutenant H. Graham Mitchell of Anacostia, Md., who didn't have a chance in the world to save himself. My plane kept flying at the same level before I was given time to open the plane cowling overhead and bail out. Imagine the frightening sensation I underwent when I realized I was too close to the ground and, now, was falling head first. I pulled out a parachute and I was amazed when it opened in time. In the next few seconds, my feet touched the land base of a mountain. Jumping seconds later, I wouldn't have made it. Although dazed, I saw Mitchell's plane burning nearby. I rushed to the scene, but he had already been ejected and killed.[13]

On 30 August a "soldier show", where soldiers performed in front of others, was given in honor of Colonel Momyer, the commanding officer of the 33rd Fighter Group. At the request of the commanding officer of the 59th Fighter Squadron, the Special Service of the 99th Fighter Squadron participated, although the men afterwards must have had mixed feelings about performing for the glory of a commander who was unfavorable towards them.

For the ground echelon, a special moment arrived. As the squadron history recounted:

> At 0900 [on 2 September] the advance echelon composed of seventy-eight enlisted men and two officers left Licata

for Milazzo, Sicily. The convoy was under the command of 1st Lieutenant Henry M. Letcher. This group remained in an assembly area until 10 September. The advance group (echelon) was split into two groups of forty persons each. The first group of thirty-nine enlisted men under the command of Lieutenant Henry M. Letcher left Milazzo by LST on the evening of 10 September. The men arrived and landed in Italy on D plus 1, 11 September. The landing was made on a beach near Battapaglia, Italy. We were under fire for twenty-four hours. The first night in Italy, the Germans broke through the Allied line. The 99th's thirty-nine men and one officer, along with the advance echelon of the 33rd Fighter Group, made a hasty retreat and were placed with elements of the British Tenth Corps. We were ordered not to fire on any German tanks, but to wait and fire upon German infantrymen should they pass where we were hidden along the highway. We came through that night successfully.

The Germans were turned back before they reached us. We had gotten out of our bivouac area in fifteen minutes. At 0600 hours the next morning we returned to bivouac area from which we had departed the night before.

That night we made another retreat approximately twenty miles south to a landing field near Paestum, Italy. The landing field which we were to have occupied was recaptured by the Germans and in moving to Paestum we passed between the German's line and elements of the 5th American Army. The enemy were less than 600 yards away from us.

Upon reaching the landing field near Paestum we were bombed at night and strafed during the day for five consecutive days. The Germans came over three times daily. We came through all of this without suffering any casualties.[14]

The pilots relocated from Licata to Termini on 4 September and then to Barcellona Pozzo di Gotto, Sicily, on 17 September. On 19 September, Sidney Brooks was scheduled to take off in his own fighter but it had a problem with the engine, so he took Dryden's plane instead. While he was taking off the engine started to splutter, so Brooks returned to the airfield to land. During the wheels-up landing, however, Brooks had failed to drop the belly tank, which sheared off on landing and bounced after the plane, eventually exploding against it. Brooks leaped from the cockpit with his smoldering flight suit and seemed to be alright, but was taken to a British field hospital just in case. He was visited by Charles Dryden later that evening:

> After supper we visited him at the hospital. He was sitting up in bed as he told us what his thoughts were during his emergency landing and how he felt fine now, and he fussed the whole time about why he had to be cooped up in a hospital.
>
> "There's nothing wrong with me," he groused. "If you guys can find my clothes, I'll leave with you!"
>
> Of course, we couldn't, and after a brief visit we left without him, but with a promise that "We'll come see you tomorrow and spring you out of here." […]
>
> Next day, true to our promise, we went to the hospital and got the shock of our lives. Sid Brooks had died during the night! The hospital spokesman told us that secondary shock and smoke inhalation that had seared Sid's lungs took his life. They showed us his body lying on a stretcher. Eyes closed.
>
> My first reaction was denial. "He can't be dead," I thought. "He doesn't look any different from the many times I saw him asleep in the cadet barracks in flight school. Surely he'll get up if I nudge him awake."
>
> Just then a fly lit on his forehead and crawled across his brow. As full of life as I had known him to be athletic, aggressive, vigorous, I expected him to brush away the pesky fly with a sweep of his hand. When he did not, I realized the truth. He was gone. I had lost a "big brother" from cadet days. I wept. When Jamie and I returned to the squadron area with the sad news, there were more than a few moist eyes. Sid Brooks had been very popular with everyone.[15]

The advance echelon had remained at Paestum with the 33rd Fighter Group, which had its own worries, as Corporal Cleveland H. Watts noted in the squadron's war diary for 1 October:

> We arose at 0600 hours and ate breakfast at 0700 hours. Despite the fact that we were not yet operating in Italy, nevertheless from force of habit we never failed to arise early. The ambulance of the 99th Fighter Squadron along with two men from the medical section were dispatched to the "line" to aid the 33rd Fighter Group. Since our invasion with the advance echelon of the 33rd Fighter Group, our ambulance "stood-by" on the line to aid them should it be necessary. The gasoline truck of the 99th Fighter Squadron was also used by the 33rd Fighter Group. Three of our men worked on this truck each day.[16]

The next day was also a good day:

> The fellow "chipped-in" and bought a hog. One of our men, who in civilian life was a butcher slaughtered and barbecued the porker. This brightened our camp life somewhat. While eating the barbecue we sat around on the ground in groups. The fellows sang many songs. Everyone went to bed that night feeling quite happy.[17]

The advance echelon spent a lot of time writing letters and taking care of themselves. It seemed that even the clerks were surprised where so much paper was acquired from, since the v-mail was rationed. Men were granted passes to visit Naples.

As Cleveland Watts narrated:

> The life of enlisted personnel of the ground crew of the US Army Air Corps is very drab at times. Occasionally they get a surprise by having something different. It may be a good movie, a personal appearance of a cinema celebrity from the United States or an extra special dinner.[18]

The advance echelon moved to Foggia airfield, where they arrived on 17 October 1943. There they were joined by the advance air echelon of the 99th Fighter Squadron. The unit was reunited again and attached to the 79th Fighter Group, consisting of the 85th, 86th, and 87th Fighter Squadrons, under the command of Colonel Earl Bates. The 99th flew missions alongside the other squadrons.

Casualties were still a concern, the results of disease or accidents. Technical Sergeant James A. Jackson died while en route to America, after leaving the combat zone of North Africa.[19] Staff Sergeant Edward Dezier died in a hospital.

Lieutenant Thomas Malone, serving with the ground echelon of the 99th Fighter Squadron, lost the use of his right arm and was transported back to the US:

> the advance of the British Eight army supported by the Negro fighter squadron, had been so rapid that the ground echelon of the 99th received orders to move up to another sector. First Lieutenant Malone and his men were instructed to get a store of vitally important supplies to a proposed advance base without delay. They realized the danger involved – that the Germans were certain to deploy troops covering their retreat. After issuing precise instructions to his men, First Lieutenant Malone set out with a small party in a cargo truck. The truck hurtled over the shell-pocked road. Suddenly the vehicle was rocked by a terrific explosion – it had set off a land mine planted by the retreating Nazis. The occupants of the truck were thrown to the ground unconscious. The officer regained consciousness while propped up in a hospital behind the lines.[20]

The supplies were delivered and on time and the mission was completed.

Momyer report

On 2 September 1943, Lieutenant Colonel Davis was ordered back to the USA to take command of the 332nd Fighter Group. Upon his departure,

Lieutenant George "Spanky" Roberts took over as commander of the 99th.

Within the air force, certain officers were advocating against the Tuskegee airmen. Other people claimed that "the American spirit of fair play" would hinder the war effort and that Black Americans were best used only as labor troops, as shown in an article that appeared in *Time* magazine on 20 September 1943:

> So little operational data on the 99th had reached Washington that it was impossible to form a conclusive opinion about its pilots. It has apparently seen little action, compared to many other units, and seems to have done fairly well; that is as far as anyone would go. But unofficial reports from the Mediterranean theater have suggested that the top air command was not altogether satisfied with the 99th's performance; there was said to be a plan some weeks ago to attach it to the Coastal Air Command, in which it would be assigned to routine convoy cover.
>
> In any case, the question of the 99th is only a single facet of one of the Army's biggest headaches: how to train and use Negro troops. No theater commander wants them in considerable numbers; the high command has trouble finding combat jobs for them. There is no lack of work to be done by Negroes as labor and engineering troops—the Army's dirty work. But the American spirit of fair play, which occasionally devotes some attention to Negro problems, would be offended by a policy of confining Negroes to such duty, and the Negro press has campaigned against it. There are plenty of Negro combat troops, but almost none of them have been tested under fire. [21]

While articles like this were detrimental to the morale of the 99th Fighter Squadron, even more damning was that commander Momyer filed a racist report, which included many negative remarks. The group did not fight as a team, he wrote, they broke formation under attack, preferred to attack undefended targets and were performing poorly.

SON OF A FAMOUS SOLDIER, YOUNG DAVIS WAS VIRTUALLY BORN TO THE ARMY— HIS FATHER IS BRIGADIER GENERAL DAVIS, HIGHEST RANKING NEGRO OFFICER IN THE U.S. ARMY!

LIEUT. COL. BENJAMIN O. DAVIS, Jr. AIR FIGHTER

COMMANDER OF THE FIRST NEGRO SQUADRON IN THE HISTORY OF THE U.S. ARMY AIR FORCE, LT. COL. DAVIS AND HIS FIGHTING PILOTS ARE IN THE THICK OF THE BLITZ AGAINST THE AXIS!

EVERY INCH A SOLDIER, DAVIS IS A WEST POINT MAN, CLASS OF '36.

A propaganda cartoon about Lieutenant Colonel Benjamin O. Davis Jr. The comic mentions that he 'was virtually born to the army', but forgets to mention that the army made it very difficult for Davis to pursue his career. (Courtesy of National Archives and Records Administration)

The report went further up the chain of command, each commander adding their own comments to it or endorsing it, and passing it up the chain. It was suggested that the 99th be assigned to coastal patrol. Lieutenant Colonel Davis was called to testify and he was the right man for the job, since he was used to being calm and composed when confronted with racism:

> On my arrival in the States, I discovered that adverse criticism had been made of the 99th's operations and the

capabilities of our pilots. Colonel Momyer had submitted a letter stating that the 99th had demonstrated insufficient air discipline and had not operated satisfactorily as a team; that its formations had disintegrated under fire; and that its pilots lacked aggressiveness. Judging from this letter, AAF officials were skeptical about how a black pilot in a P-40 would react when anti-aircraft fire burst about his ship or when an enemy was strewing cannon shells and machine gun bullets around his cockpit. The courage of our pilots and their ability to maintain their composure under fire were being called into question.

The major thrust of Momyer's report was that the unit should be removed from combat operations and relegated to the sterile and monotonous mission of coastal patrol. This recommendation was endorsed through channels by Maj. Gen. Edwin J. House, Major General Cannon, and Lieutenant General Spaatz. General Spaatz's endorsement stated that the 99th had been given a fair test in combat. Another endorsement remarked, "The Negro type has not the proper reflexes to make a first-class fighter pilot," a definite throwback to the 1925 War College report, which had referred to anthropological literature placing blacks lower on the scale of human evolution than whites because of their "smaller cranium, lighter brain, [and] cowardly and immoral character."

Upon receipt of Momyer's report, the commanding general of the AAF, Henry H. ("Hap") Arnold, recommended to Gen. George C. Marshall, the Army Chief of Staff, that the 99th be removed from tactical operations; that the 332nd Fighter Group, when ready for deployment, be sent to a non-combat area; and that the then current AAF plan to activate a black bombardment group, the 477th, be abandoned. In the minds of the commanders of the Mediterranean theater and the AAF, the "experiment" was over, and blacks had demonstrated their expected inability to perform in combat at the required level of proficiency.

I was furious. Momyer's criticism was completely unwarranted and unreasonable, and surely the details should have been brought to my attention at the time the alleged deficiencies were observed. By mid-September, I had quieted down sufficiently to hold a press conference at the Pentagon, where I went to some length to tell the story of the 99th from the time I had assumed command until my return to the States. I stressed that the Army Air Corps had looked upon the 99th as an experiment that would have to prove that blacks could be taught to fly airplanes to its standards, and that blacks could operate effectively as a team in combat. In retrospect, it seems ridiculous that as late as 1943, the AAF still believed that the utilization of black men as pilots had to be regarded as an experiment. But the same kind of backward thinking had inspired the racist 1925 War College report, and many otherwise capable and reasonable senior AAF leaders continued to believe that blacks could not possibly qualify as combat pilots, in spite of what the 99th had already accomplished.[22]

The report of the committee was edited by Colonel Emmett O'Donnell and he included a memo, recommending to reconsider the entire subject. The president would certainly not appreciate the report, as it showed a lack of understanding of the contemporary problems. Furthermore, the fallout of the report would damage the morale of the Black American people. As the colonel concluded, "it might be far better to let the entire matter drop, without any letter to the President."[23]

In the end, it was decided that no further action would be taken, unless all P-40 units in the area were examined. A few factors needed to be taken into account. The 99th had received fewer pilots than the white units and the 99th had been assigned to ground attack sorties, leaving them fewer opportunities to confront the Luftwaffe. The opening statement of this report summarized it well: "An examination of the record of the 99th Fighter Squadron reveals no significant general difference between this squadron and the balance of the P-40 squadrons in the Mediterranean Theatre Operations."[24]

Chapter 3

Making progress

The 332nd Fighter Group and three squadrons

The 100th Fighter Squadron was briefly active in December 1941 and it was inactivated a few months later. It was activated the second time in October 1942, with Captain James Hunter in command. On 26 January 1943 Lieutenant Mac Ross was commanding officer of the 100th Fighter Squadron and the unit was rapidly built up. On 5 April, George Knox became the commanding officer of the 100th Fighter Group and a week later it moved to Selfridge Field, Michigan. On 29 June, Lieutenant Elwood Driver took over as commander, and on 6 July, First Lieutenant Robert Tresville (previously in charge of the 302nd Fighter Squadron) became the commanding officer. Training continued steadily, and on 22 December the unit departed Selfridge Field.

On 13 October 1942 the 301st Fighter Squadron was activated at Tuskegee. The squadron had no personnel assigned, so it was not until 12 December, when the first soldiers arrived, that the unit got off the ground. More soldiers followed and on 26 December the first officer arrived, Second Lieutenant William M. Womack. He would become the unit's first Adjutant. By the end of December, the unit had 134 enlisted men and one officer. More enlisted men and officers arrived in January 1943, including First Lieutenant Frederick E. Miles as a commander. First Lieutenant Charles DeBow took over as commanding officer on 26 January. The unit continued to expand in February 1943.

On 23 March, the unit received orders to move from Tuskegee and proceed to Selfridge field Michigan, where it would train for combat duties. The unit left on the 27th and arrived on the 29th. By the end of march, the unit consisted of 354 enlisted men and fifteen officers.

On 3 May, the unit moved to Oscoda Army Air Field, Michigan. Training was intensified in this period. Inclement weather meant ground school, "but when it was clear, every effort was made to get as many planes into the air for as long a period of time as was possible."[1]

On 9 May, the unit suffered its first casualty. Lieutenant Wilmeth Sidat-Singh bailed out of his plane over Lake Huron after suffering an engine failure. However, his parachute became entangled in the plane and he went down in the crash. His body was recovered in the second half of June.

As the squadron history recounts about June 1943: "Items of interest outside of regular squadron duties were nil for month of June. The training program was in full swing, and every man was doing his utmost to get it over with."[2]

> Our first period of training at Oscoda was fast drawing to a close as the month of July opened. With the help of a very efficient ground grew, the pilots had been able to get an enormous amount of time in the air and through their excellent marksmanship, had been able to set a few records in Aerial Gunnery, but for the most part, they were tired and anxious to see their training at Oscoda completed.[3]

Some of the men were transferred from the unit and placed on readiness for overseas duty.

On 9 July, the training at Oscoda ended and the ground echelon departed by truck in the morning for Selfridge Field. The pilots arrived the next day.

On 25 September, two new officers were assigned to the 301st squadron: Second Lieutenants Claybourne A. Lockett and Johnson C. Wells. Three days later, Johnson C. Wells was killed when his plane hit telegraph wires while attempting a forced landing.

The squadron history summarized November: "The month of November saw very little of interest happening within the squadron."[4] The unit relocated to Oscoda Army Air Base on the 9th and returned to Selfridge Field on the 19th.

The last squadron in the 332nd Fighter Group was the 302nd Fighter Squadron. It was activated on 13 October 1942 at Tuskegee Army Flying School, Alabama. It moved from there on 27 March 1943 to Selfridge

Field, and from 9 November 1943 to 29 December, was stationed at Oscoda Army Air Field. Edward Gleed was the commanding officer.

On 22 December 1943, a train left from Oscoda Field with the men of the 100th, the 301st, and the 302nd Fighter Squadron on board. Under the guidance of Benjamin O. Davis, these three squadrons would go towards Europe.

As the 302nd Fighter Squadron's history recounted:

> Long before December 1943 there had been rumors that the 332nd Fighter Group was destined to soon depart for overseas duty. During the month of December those rumors probed to be well founded. Inspections occurred day after day until all equipment for foreign service had been issued. When that was completed all conceived that it was only a matter of days or hours when Lieutenant Gleed would tell us: "This is it". That time arrived on December 20, but proved to be a dry run. But on December 22 the 302nd departed Selfridge Field, Michigan, for "destination unknown". There was on the night of departure the usual band music, and in addition the 302nd was awarded a proficiency medal by the post commander which was an incentive for all men of the squadron to continue the excellent performances of the past, wherever they might be sent in the service of their country.[5]
>
> On the morning of December 25, the squadron arrived at Camp Patrick Henry, Hampton Roads Port of Embarkation Area. This was indeed a strange Christmas morning for the men of the squadron. There was very little talk concerning the holiday season but I am sure that the thoughts of every man of the squadron were with those they were leaving behind.[6]

The 99th Fighter Squadron in Italy – 1943

Flying with the 79th Fighter Group, the 99th Fighter Squadron got a lot of valuable experience. They were trained in close cover support for ground troops. Many operations were made to support the British Eighth Army. Veterans of the Pantellerian and Sicilian Campaigns, the pilots of the 99th Fighter Squadron considered themselves experienced. The 79th Fighter Group, however, had a lot more experience and their tactics were better than those of the 99th. The flying formation in enemy territory changed, as well as the 99th's system for take-off.

In the second half of October 1943 the 99th attacked shipping targets in the region of Isernia-Capionne and was free to engage road traffic northwest of Sangro. On 22 October the unit attacked German ammunition dumps and two of the P-40Ls were damaged by flak. The Luftwaffe was absent, while the squadron flew beach control and armed reconnaissance.

In November the weather changed and life on the ground became more arduous as mud seeped into the tents. The change in weather also made flying more dangerous. The 99th continued to fly many missions and on 22 November James Wiley became the first member of the squadron to complete fifty missions.

On 1 November, around fifty P-38s landed on Sal Sola airfield, part of the Foggia airfield complex. Mechanics of the 99th Fighter Squadron serviced twenty of them. There was good cooperation with the four squadrons of the 79th Fighter Group.

Pilots of the 307th Fighter Squadron as well as a member of the 99th Fighter Squadron in Italy on 2 February 1944. (Courtesy of National Archives and Records Administration)

A Jeep with pilots of the 307th Fighter Squadron as well as a member of the 99th Fighter Squadron in Italy on 2 February 1944 alongside a supermarine 'Spitfire' at an airfield near Nettuno, Italy. (Courtesy of National Archives and Records Administration)

On 3 November, Lieutenant H. Clarks hit a P-38 that was taxiing towards the runway. The landing gear on the right side of Clarks' plane was damaged, but the lieutenant continued with his mission and after dropping his bombs, he crashed on his homefield.

The first men of the ground echelon arrived on 7 November, with more following shortly afterwards. The weather turned so bad that several tents were blown away by the wind on the 13th, and between the 13th and 17th, the squadron were unable to fly any missions.

The unit moved up to Madna, near Termoli on 19 November and more missions followed. The pilots settled in at Madna field. Corporal Cleveland H. Watts, when writing about the battalion in the month of November, conveys the problems quite well:

> The mud is black, sticky, and slippery. [...] We are up to our necks in mud. Here and there are fallen tents, blown the night before by the wind. Not one soldier has on a complete uniform. Every man has a different idea regarding which of his clothing to wear in order to keep warm. It is very difficult to keep clothes clean.[7]

Mechanics working on a P-40 of the 99th Fighter Squadron. (Courtesy of National Archives and Records Administration)

On 9 December 1943, General Arnold told Captain George Roberts that the eyes of Black America were upon the 99th Fighter Squadron. Now it was the task of the squadron to not disappoint those people.[8] On 13 December Lawrence Boisseau died from injuries that he had sustained in a motor accident.

Morale was rather low. Mud and rain complicated matters, while the Luftwaffe remained absent. However, the inclement weather, the dangerous missions against ground targets and the toll of combat were felt by the men of the squadron. To waste no words on the ever-present enemy, Jim Crow. As the squadron war diary recounted:

> we have become accustomed to its surroundings, the mud, the sea, and the snowcapped mountains to the north east of Madna field. Occasionally the sun is bright, the mud becomes dry. It is then that the soldiers mark time against

The ground crew of the 99th Fighter Squadron prepare a P-40 for a mission in Italy, 30 December 1943. (Courtesy of National Archives and Records Administration)

the weather in order to get clothing washed. A few days later, rain has again whipped the ground into slush. This goes on week after week.[9]

The first two weeks of January consisted of close air support given to the British 8th Army. The pilots bombed and strafed in the assistance of the troops on the ground.

John Morgan was tragically killed on 2 January 1944 while attempting to land his P-40; unable to stop, his plane ended up in a ditch. On 15 January, while divebombing the town of San Valentino, Lieutenant William Griffin's plane went missing – last seen smoking and diving at 2,000ft. It turned out that he had made a crash landing in hostile territory and spent the rest of the war as a prisoner of war. On 16 January the squadron moved to Capodichino airfield.

Meanwhile, the 99th Fighter Squadron was under close scrutiny. This was not just from the Allies, but from the Axis as well. In a Danish broadcast, made by a German propaganda station on 22 January 1944, the 99th Fighter Squadron and the *Time* article were mentioned:

US NEGRO PILOTS MAKE POOR SHOWING

The US naturally wanted to spare American lives as much as possible by making use of Negroes, but the Negroes had become too enlightened to be willing to accept the honor of becoming cannon fodder in a struggle from which they would derive slight benefit.

Negro Fighter Squadron: Nonetheless there existed the 99th Fighter Squadron consisting solely of Negroes, and commanded by a Negro, named Lt. Col. Davis. This squadron was created for propaganda purposes in order to lure Negroes by a grand uniform, good pay, slight personal risk, and by hinting that Negro pilots would be on a basis of equality. The uniform and the suggestion of equality made a definite impression, and the squadron was created. It appears, however, from a speech made by Lt. Col. Davis that this equality has been somewhat lacking, and this Davis demanded in strong terms.

On Atlantic Coast: The magazine, TIME, in this connection pointed out that the 99th squadron had not contributed satisfactory results on the Mediterranean front. The US Command had then in mind the withdrawing of this squadron from all areas where they might come into contact with the German Air Force, and instead put it to convoy work on the American coast.

Chance for Equality: This problem concerning Negroes was solved in the last war by putting Negro soldiers to do labor service, but the Negroes were not satisfied with this arrangement. A "leading Negro paper" stresses the fact that this war is the American Negroes' great chance to put through their demand for equality. This sounded threatening and did not, of course, help relations between blacks and whites in the US.[10]

German propaganda tried to flare up the racial tensions in America. The aspirations were that racial tensions would hinder the American war effort. However, soon the 99th Fighter Squadron would prove what they were worth to America and to the Luftwaffe.

27 January 1944

On 22 January, the same day as the German radio broadcast, the Allied landings at Anzio took place. Intended to circumvent the German troops holding out at the Gustav Line, the idea was to land Allied troops along the coast and thus enable a push towards Rome in the north. However, the coastal assault quickly became bogged down. The Luftwaffe showed themselves again and the 99th could now engage them, being employed as cover for the ground elements.

Members of the 99th Fighter Squadron pose for a picture at the Anzio beachhead. (Courtesy of National Archives and Records Administration)

This was done on 27 January, with spectacular results, as the squadron war diary recounted:

> On 27 January 1944, while on patrol in the assault area south of Rome, our formation led by Captain Clarence C. Jamison, spotted fifteen FW-190s at 08:40 hours dive bombing our shipping off Peter Beach. Our formation of sixteen aircraft went into the attack diving down on the enemy. Lieutenants Baugh and Allen attacked one FW-190 from 5,000ft. About four five-second bursts sent the FW-190 crashing at F-8250. Lieutenant Baugh then turned left and fired three three-second bursts, 10-degree deflection shots on another FW-190. Tracers were seen going into the plane and small fragments flew off from the wing and tail. Lieutenant Ashley, jumped one FW-190 on deck and chased him to within a few miles of Rome. The FW-190 first began to smoke and burst into flames. Lieutenant Roberts chased one FW-190 on deck to F-7662 and the FW-190 flopped over on his back and went into the ground. Lieutenant Toppins, #3 man in Red Flight, fired short bursts into an FW-190 heading in the general direction of Rome. As the plane was smoking excessively and diving toward the ground about 50ft, a probably is claimed by Lt. Toppins.
>
> Lieutenant McCrumby at 5,000ft spotted an FW-190 on deck. Lt. McCrumby picked a lead and commenced firing at point blank range. Sections of the horizontal stabilizer and rudder flew off.
>
> Lt. Deiz, got a 60-degree deflection shot closing 150 to 200 yards on an FW-190 below. A portion of the cowling flew off and the plane went into a steep dive at 750ft and crashed and burned in a yard near a house in patrol area.
>
> Lt. Perry caught one FW-190 coming out of a dive, raking the enemy ship from head to tail about 300 yards. The FW-190 was at 1,000 to 1,500ft when pieces from the canopy flew off. The plane fluttered and fell off on the wing and headed for the ground.

Captain Lemuel R. Custis (left) and Charles B. Hall, of the 99th Fighter Squadron. (Courtesy of National Archives and Records Administration)

Major Roberts, commanding officer of the squadron, chased an FW-190 to F-7555, hits were registered in the right wing and chunks flew off. Major Roberts' ship was hit by flak which knocked a hole in his wing cutting his electrical that side. His three guns stopped firing. The Major headed for home, sighted a machine gun nest and with his three remaining guns and his wingman strafed the nest.[11]

The three guns on the right wing stopped firing, due to the hole in his wing and the electrical system was also affected.

However, the day was not over yet and as the squadron history recounted:

At 14:25 hours on the afternoon of 27 January 1944 Captain Custis, crafty leader spotted an FW-190. The FW-190 was on deck. Several bursts were fired at close range in the fuselage. The plane crashed in a creek.

Lieutenant Bailey caught an FW-190 headed in the general direction of Rome and with a 45-degree deflection shot. The pilot was seen to bail out.

Lieutenant Eagleson caught an FW-190 diving on the tail of Lieutenant Lawrence. He closed in to 250 yards firing a 10-degree deflection shot. The FW-190 burst into flames and crashed at F-8558.

Lt. Lawrence probably destroyed an FW-190 at F-8725 with a 75-degree deflection shot. Lieutenant Eagleson saw the FW-190 roll over and dive for the ground smoking excessively at 3,000ft.

Lt. Lane was shot down during his chase on two FW-190s Lieutenant Lane's ship caught fire, his cockpit became unbearably hot. Lt. Lane bailed out and was picked up by Fifth Army troops in the assault area. He was flown back to our field in a Piper Cub.[12]

The day would not be without casualties however. Allen Lane was forced to jump out of his plane after it was riddled with bullets, and Sam Bruce, who had survived the accident in which Graham Mitchell was killed, was last seen chasing a pair of FW-190s. Needing to abandon his plane, he jumped out, but his parachute did not fill. His body was discovered later. He never got the chance to meet his daughter, who was born the following month. Also that day, Lieutenant Gibson landed his damaged plane in a belly landing. He had been hit by the enemy.

The next day yielded good results. According to the squadron history, on 28 January 1944 a flight commanded by Charles B. Hall was flying above the beaches, when:

> [he] sighted seven-plus enemy aircraft approaching our shipping from the north. Our formation at 5,000ft dove on the enemy as he turned away. One Me-109 was shot down by Captain Hall at F-7240 by a 15-degree deflection shot closing in at 300 yards. The Me-109 was on deck and burst into flames crashing on the ground.
>
> Captain Hall caught an FW-190 at F-8146 firing dead astern closing in at 200 yards with short bursts. The FW-190 went into the ground. Lieutenant Smith caught an FW-190 at F-8339 about 3,000ft, with a 30-degree deflection shot above and behind to the left. The pilot was seen to bail out. One of our ships was damaged by enemy aircraft. All returned and landed safely.[13]

According to the squadron history, they destroyed twelve aircraft, got three probables and damaged four more. It provided a boost, also for the other squadrons. As Colonel Davis, the commander of the 332nd Fighter Group recounted:

> We immediately received news of the 99th's aerial victories over the Anzio beachhead on 27 and 28 January, just days before our landing. This came as a tremendous shot in the arm. The glamour of a quick succession of aerial victories immediately produced a wave of recognition for the 99th and other black airmen in the theater. No number of bombs expertly placed on ground targets or in support of ground troops could have produced comparable acclaim.[14]

Captain Charles B. Hall. (Courtesy of Ike Skelton Combined Arms Research Library Digital Library)

Pilots of the 99th Fighter Squadron talk about the day's exploits. (Courtesy of National Archives and Records Administration)

The fight continues

As January rolled into February, the squadron history recalls:

> What at first appeared to be routine patrol missions for pilots
> of the 99th Fighter Squadron have developed into lively
> engagements with the enemy. The use of the word lively is
> not to be misunderstood for many of these missions have been
> major encounters with Jerry, some being successful for the
> flyers of the 99th, others being rather disastrous inasmuch as
> some of the famed pilots of the 99th Fighter Squadron failed
> to return from some of these missions. In the short time of
> three weeks the experiences of the 99th Fighter Squadron
> pilots have become important lessons either to be passed
> on to less experienced and younger pilots, to be utilized by
> themselves on future missions, or to ever remain with them.
> Each mission has become (for the pilots) a struggle for
> survival and a blow toward eliminating the enemy.[15]

The patrol missions continued on 2 February, but nothing happened. On 3 February a flight of eight FW-190s was seen, but as the 99th Fighter Squadron attempted to engage them, the German planes turned into the clouds and disappeared. Both sides pushed at each other's lines and employed aircraft to break the enemy's resistance. Two days later, another patrol was in the skies over Anzio.

On the first mission of that day, seven of the 99th Fighter Squadron pilots tangled with German aircraft. While patrolling over the beachhead, more than ten FW-190s dove out of the sun, their target: the harbor at Anzio. The seven pilots engaged the German aircraft; Lieutenant Elwood T. Driver caught one of the FWs and closed to within 300 yards. Flames were seen coming out of the right sight. As Elwood Driver explained:

> About ten plus FW-190s dove from 16,000ft from an easterly direction and flattened out on deck over Anzio. At the time, I was headed west at 6,000ft. Before the FW-190 reached a position beneath me, I made a diving left turn and pulled out about 300 yards behind him and began firing. I continued to fire in long bursts even though he was pulling away. As my traces straddled the cockpit, a sheet of flames burst from the right side. I last saw the plane burning and headed toward Rome at 50ft from the ground. The firing was done from 500ft down the deck. I was slightly above at all times. During the time I was firing, a clipped wing Spitfire was also firing. He was to my right and ahead about 50 yards.[16]

Clarence Jamison and George McCrumby also tangled with FW-190s; McCrumby describes being hit:

> Something hit underneath the ship, then another burst cracked the side of my cockpit, plunging the plane into a dive at 4,000ft. I tried to pull out but had no control. The elevators had been knocked out. I had no alternative but to jump. I tried the left side, but the slipstream knocked me back. Then I tried the right side and got halfway out, when again the slipstream threw me against the fuselage. I struggled until all but my right foot was free and dangled

from the diving plane until the wind turned the ship at about 1,000ft and shook me loose. I reached for the rip cord six times before finding it, but my parachute opened immediately, landing me safely in a cow pasture.[17]

Clarence Jamison had slightly more luck. He was chasing five FW-190s when his machine guns stopped firing. He was fired on, and hit by, the FW-190s before he could escape; being too low to jump out of his plane, he belly landed in an open field instead. Immediately after landing, a group of American soldiers motioned to him to get away from his downed aircraft as soon as possible. The Germans were only a few hundred yards away. The soldiers escorted him to their headquarters and from there Jamison made his way back to the squadron.

More engagements in the skies over Anzio followed. On 7 February 1944, three FW-190s were shot down. Clinton B. Mills, Leonard Jackson, and Wilson Eagleson each shot one down. Clinton Mills recounted of this event:

We were patrolling the beachhead when suddenly about 20 FW 190s dropped out of the clouds and began dive bombing our landing troops. My flight of P-40s caught the last flight of four Jerries as they released their bombs and leveled off.

I was in a hard bank when I caught one of the Nazis in my sights and blasted a 30-degree directional burst at him. I hit his cowling and as his engine started burning, he whipped over into a tight spin.

The pilot bailed out and I followed him down to see if he'd land behind our lines. However, a lucky (for him) gust of wind carried him to about 20 miles behind enemy lines.[18]

On 8 February six P-40s provided an escort to Nettuno and back for the DC-3 of Lieutenant General Mark Clark, commanding officer of the Fifth Army.

The patrol and bombing missions continued throughout the month. On 13 February, a detachment of the 99th Fighter Squadron arrived from Madna Landing Ground. They had been separated since 15 January, when the squadron departed for Capodichino airfield. On 19 February Lieutenant Gibson made a forced landing at the Anzio beachhead.

One of the most traumatic days for the squadron was 21 February – the day started with an accident. While on patrol, Alwayne Dunlap's Warhawk started to smoke and then flames erupted from his aircraft. Dunlap tried to land on the beach head, but overshot the field. He tried to turn, but the plane, still smoking and burning, stalled and crashed.

An oil leak posed a problem for Lieutenant Bailey. His visibility was obscured by the oil smear over the canopy and he needed to land. Lieutenant Herbert's plane was hit by flak and Lieutenant Houston made a belly landing near Nettuno. Lieutenant Saunders was reported as missing in action, but it later turned out he had crash landed and was in the hospital. No claims were submitted, despite fierce fighting with German aircraft.

On 27 February, the service detachment arrived from Madna Field. On 29 February, a mission took off. Lieutenant McCrumby, who had bailed out of his airplane a little over a month ago, reported engine trouble and turned back toward the airfield. He did not report back so two pilots, Colonel Bates, of the 79th Fighter Group and Lieutenant Lawson, took off to find him. Sadly, they were unable to locate him and on 15 July 1945, McCrumby was declared dead.

The mood had been tense. Sickness plagued the outfit. The mechanics worked hard to keep the unit flying. The pilots were on edge and made fewer jokes while waiting for take-off. Inclement weather limited flying operations. On 3 March, the squadron history noted, "it rained the entire day. […] The rain has made slush of the ground especially where there is considerable transportation to and fro." If the weather allowed it, missions were flown. During one of these missions, a B-17 was seen on fire, crashing down. Five people with parachutes managed to get out.

This changed on 8 March, when the squadron received three P-47s. The P-47 Thunderbolt was the plane also flown by the other squadrons of the 79th Fighter Group. It made the men think that they would remain with the 79th, because now they would have the same planes. Pilots off duty made transitional flights in the Thunderbolts to familiarize themselves with the aircraft.

On 9 March, the squadron performed two dive bombing missions. The first one was at three-gun positions to the north of Anzio. The planes all returned safely. The second mission of that day ran into trouble. The visibility was poor, but the pilots were believed to have silenced the guns. While over the target, there was a lot of anti-aircraft fire and Lieutenant Houston was forced to land his plane at the Nettuno beach head. This would be the third time in less than a month that Houston landed an aircraft in the area. He returned to his airbase in another plane, which had been abandoned at the beach after being damaged by flak in the coolant system. Lieutenant John Hamilton was wounded in his leg by flak, but returned home safely.

Staff Sergeant McGary L. Edwards, Crew Chief in the 99th Fighter Squadron photographed working on a P-40 "Warhawk" in Italy on 23 March 1944. (Courtesy of National Archives and Records Administration)

In the night of the 14 to 15 March, the base was bombed by German aircraft. As Cleveland Watts, the soldier in charge of the squadron's war diary wrote:

> During the night enemy aircraft raised hell for thirty minutes. It was one of the worst air raids we had witnessed since being overseas. Anti-aircraft guns blazed away at the fleeing German planes. From a window of a blacked-out room of a school building in Casavatore, Italy, this writer watched the rays of giant searchlights as they searched the sky for enemy planes. No bombs fell near the school building in which the enlisted men of the 99th Fighter Squadron lived.[19]

During the day two missions were flown, both against a target near Monte Cassino, where the famous monastery used to be.

On 17 March, Mount Vesuvius erupted. It spewed ash and debris in all directions, severely hampering operations for the days to come. As the squadron history recounted,

> Mount Vesuvius is spreading havoc among civilians and soldiers. Vesuvius has begun to erupt. It is traveling at the rate of 300 yards per hour. In places the crest of the creeping lava was fifty feet high. […] We are seeing everything by being in the army.[20]

It would continue to spew ash and debris into the skies. Two men, Sergeant Alexander Buchanon and Corporal Clarence Kimes helped with the evacuation of troops and civilians in areas threatened by the lava.

On 19 March, the 99th took out an 'Anzio Express' rail gun. The beaches were harassed by a railway gun that shelled them. Eight P-40s were sent out to locate tunnel openings, where the gun might be hidden. They dropped bombs on a suspected tunnel and closed it. One P-40 was damaged, but the 'Express' ceased harassing the frontline troops.

The air raids were something that the unit became accustomed to. As the squadron war diary records on 25 March:

> There was one air raid last night by enemy aircraft. It was one of many the 99th Fighter Squadron have experienced since being in the Napoli area. Most of the men had retired. They did not bother to arise, nor did they become excited. From a cot, this writer watched the tracers of Allied anti-aircraft guns go up after Jerry.[21]

On 30 March, during the second mission of the day, Lieutenant Sloan was wounded by hostile anti-aircraft fire. Both plane and pilot were struck. He crash landed his plane in friendly territory and was picked up by New Zealand soldiers, before being taken to the hospital.

On 1 April the remaining three P-47s were transferred to the 85th Fighter Squadron, which was also attached to the 79th Fighter Group. Rumors circulated that the 99th was going to be detached from the 79th Fighter Group and many people hoped that this would not be true.

There was considerable grumbling and complaining when the men received word the next day that they were to be attached to the 324th Fighter Group. Activated on 6 July 1942, this fighter group consisted of the 314th, the 315th, and the 316th Fighter Squadron. The unit also flew with the P-40 Warhawk. The soldiers of the 99th were proud of their attachment to the 79th Fighter Group. As a sign of the close relation that the pilots of the 99th Fighter Squadron had with the pilots of the 79th Fighter Group, a farewell party was given in Naples by the pilots of the 99th. This was attended by many officers the three white squadrons, as well as Colonel Bates, the group commander.

Also, on that day the squadron moved to Cercola airfield, where it was attached to the 324th Fighter Group. The dust at the new airfield was a problem for both pilots and planes. Operating from the Cercola airfield brought back memories of the airfield at Fardjouna in North Africa, where there was also sand, dust and scattered trees.

On 3 April, Staff Sergeant Eugene Pickett, a member of Engineering Section, was killed. He had been shot and died en route to the hospital.

He was buried two days later. An investigator would stop by to uncover the mystery surrounding Pickett's death.

The first combat mission from Cercola was conducted on 4 April. Twelve planes took off to dive-bomb an enemy motor park near Frasati. One aircraft was damaged and another nosed over on landing. The dust posed a considerable problem.

Easter, 9 April 1944, was just another day for the men of the squadron, although some of the enlisted men were invited to dinner by their Italian friends. It was the second Easter away from home and the unit flew two dive bombing missions.

On 20 April, Lieutenant General Ira Eaker, the commander of the Mediterranean Allied Air Forces, visited the 99th Fighter Squadron. With him came Lieutenant Colonel Davis, commander of the 332nd Fighter Group. To meet them was Colonel Lydon, commanding officer of the 324th Fighter Group. General Eaker talked for about an hour to the men and the reporters present. Before he departed, many soldiers took a picture with the General, about whom they had read a lot. The same day another mission was conducted against a gun position. One aircraft, flown by Lieutenant Gibson, crash landed at Castel Volturno, but he was unhurt.

On 24 April, the squadron had two missions, and one of them was a close call. Shortly after taking off, Lieutenant Jamison returned to land his plane. He did not jettison his 500-pound bomb and the twelve 20-lb fragmentation bombs until he was 25ft above the runway.

Other pilots also experienced problems. Lieutenant Daniels's plane nosed over on landing, and Lieutenant Brown had to jettison his bomb before landing at an airbase in the vicinity of Santa Maria.

During the celebration of the squadron's first anniversary overseas, hostile aircraft came over to visit. Flares bracketed the entire area of Cercola. Many men jumped into foxholes, and in the searchlights the men could see bombs being dropped on Naples.

As the month of April came to a close, the squadron's diary noted:

> The attitudes of enlisted men are such that it is difficult to accurately describe the degree of their morale. The link connecting the state of morale of enlisted men with

performance of duty, has developed into an unbelievable pride in organization, which pride acts as an incentive toward understanding more fully that a war is being fought and they, the enlisted men are in the midst of it; therefore, anything that might affect the normalcy of the status of morale among enlisted men of the 99th Fighter Squadron is hidden behind love and admiration for their squadron.[22]

The last day of April ended with the best mission of the month so far. Seven planes took off to engage a dump near Avezzano, Italy. As the squadron's diary noted:

> All bombs hit within the target area. Large fires resulted, black some and red flames rose to 1,000ft. One building in the target area was demolished, another was left smoking. Gas drums in the target area were strafed, however, the drums did not explode. A gas truck on a road in the town of Avezzano, Italy, was strafed. The truck blew up and three plus personnel were killed. Three fright cars were observed on a side track. These cars were strafed, no fires were started, however the cars were damaged. Flak near the target area was heavy, intense and accurate. All seven aircraft returned safely to their home landing ground.[23]

During a mission on 10 May, the only thing of significance that happened, was that eight P-40s were followed for a short distance by four Spitfires that had taken off shortly before. On 10 May the unit had moved to Pignataro Maggiore Airfield, where missions continued to disrupt hostile reinforcements, break enemy points of resistance and prevent them from bringing up supplies. During a strafing mission on 27 May, three of the eight aircraft did not return. Lieutenant Smith landed at Nettuno after an ammunition box on his wing caught fire. Lieutenant Mills likewise landed later at Nettuno. Lieutenant James Brown jumped out of a smoking plane and although he landed among several trees; he is listed as killed.

Lieutenant Theodore A. Wilson, member of the 99th Fighter Squadron, rolls his parachute after successfully bailing out of his P-40 after it was hit by flak on 3 May 1944. (Courtesy of National Archives and Records Administration)

The last month as a separate squadron

In June most of the missions were intended to hamper the enemy. Supply lines were disrupted by dive bombing and road blocks hindered the enemy further. This kind of action directly contributed to successes at the front.

Rome fell to the Allies on 4 June. That same day, thirty-four motor vehicles were damaged and ten other vehicles were destroyed, three oil tankers among. Twelve people were killed and one 20 mm machine gun was silenced. The 99th Fighter Squadron was assigned to the Twelfth Tactical Air Command from 5 June to 10 June.

On 5 June, three eight-plane combat missions were conducted. The first mission destroyed three vehicles. The second spotted around 150 transport vehicles north of Rome, damaging twenty-five of them and destroying ten, including a motor-cycle. The last flight destroyed fourteen motor transports and damaged two more.

On 6 June, the Allied landings took place in Normandy, France. That same day the 99th performed six missions in groups of four. In total twenty-nine vehicles were damaged, eleven destroyed, as well as a motorcycle. Two pilots of the 99th had to make crash landings; Lieutenant Dart was fortunate to crash land in friendly territory and return to the unit swiftly. Lieutenant Leonard Jackson landed in territory that had been abandoned by the Germans only two hours earlier. He did manage to capture two prisoners however, and returned to camp the next day.

On 7 June, the 99th Fighter Squadron performed four missions, with four airplanes on each mission. Forty-seven vehicles were damaged and another twenty-four destroyed. A self-propelled gun was also knocked out. Since the enemy used vehicles to bring up supplies and reinforcements, the destruction of said means was a boon for the soldiers at the front.

After they had performed their dive-bombing mission on 8 June, Howard Baugh and Lewis Smith spotted a German convoy. While engaging it, they flew parallel to the road, resulting in Smith's aircraft being hit. He jumped out of his stricken plane and descended to earth with his parachute. He would spend the rest of the war as a prisoner of war.

The 99th was briefly attached to the 86th Fighter Group from 11 June, and that same day it moved to the Campiano Airfield.

On 14 June, Lieutenant Clarence W. Allen was shot down. After being hit by flak, he landed around 50 yards from a highway. German soldiers from a nearby gun position tried to capture him, but he managed to evade them, hiding in a wooded area; the Germans fired indiscriminately at the area, hoping to hit him. Towards nightfall, Allen covered himself with leaves so that the Germans would not be able to find him – they were so close that he could hear them talking. Fortunately, the enemy departed during the night, and the next morning Allen found a French armored unit and made his way back to the 99th.[24]

The 99th relocated once more, going to Orbetello Airfield on 17 June. On 23 June Howard L. Baugh accidentally shot himself and needed to be taken to the hospital. On 29 June, Floyd A. Thompson was taken prisoner.

On 30 June, the 99th was assigned to the 332nd Fighter Group. Davis wrote about this:

> Later I was to learn that the 99th would not join the 332nd
> until an intensive 12th Air Force tactical operation had been

completed in May. General Cannon wanted to retain the 99th's tactical expertise until the May operation had been completed. He regarded the 99th as his most hardened and experienced P-40 unit and wanted it for pinpoint dive-bombing missions close to our frontline troops.[25]

[...]

Shortly before the 99th joined the 332nd, it experienced a humorous yet dangerous incident. For a long time, a ranking enlisted mechanic, Technical Sergeant Henry Cornell, had wanted to fly a P-40. One memorable day he warmed up a P-40, bent forward in the tiny cockpit, attached a sheet of instructions to the instrument panel, taxied to the end of the takeoff strip, and with a green light from the control tower, roared down the runway and leaped into the air in a steep climb. The news spread like wildfire among the mechanics, pilots who happened to be on the flying line, and others, none of whom could take their eyes off the crew chief. In the plane, Sergeant Cornell referred to the instructions on the panel to remind himself of the sequence of actions he must perform to get the P-40 back on the ground. When he opened the canopy as part of the prelanding procedure, however, the wind blew his instructions away, and the daring sergeant was at his loss as to his next move. He did recall reading that he should lower the landing flaps, but when he did, he lost so much airspeed that the plane stalled and crashed nose first on the approach to the runway.

The humor of the incident was lost on those in the chain of command, because of the loss of a combat airplane. Sergeant Cornell never achieved his heartfelt desire for flight training in the Army Air Forces, but he had experienced the flight of his life and satisfied once and for all his belief that he really could fly a P-40. Fortunately, only his feelings were hurt.[26]

Chapter 4

The 332nd Fighter Group in Italy

Three squadrons in Italy

The 332nd Fighter Group had been deemed ready for overseas service by the end of 1943. After having received orders to go across the ocean, the mood among the men was tense. As the 302nd Fighter Squadron diary noted:

> After more of the same type of inspection previously encountered the squadron was pronounced ready for the great adventure. On the morning of January 3, the squadron boarded the train for the final ride to the port of embarkation. The morale of the men was high and there was little outward evidence of the emotions which must have been mingling in the hearts and minds of the mean. The squadron boarded the liberty ship *T.B. Robinson* and on the afternoon of January 4 the voyage began. There was soon proof that we were part of a great convoy which quieted the fears of many of the men.[1]

It embarked on ships to cross the Atlantic. As the 301st Fighter Squadron history noted:

> The first days out, the sea was fairly rough, and most of our men were confined to their bunks because of certain green pallor about their gills. After those first few days though, the sea calmed down, and we were able to enjoy fairly decent weather for the remainder of our voyage. When we were about seventy miles off the African coast, we got our first and only "sub" scare. Destroyer Escort vessels began

dodging in and out of the convoy dropping depth charges, indiscriminately or, at least, it seemed so to us. We never did see any evidence of a sub, but anyway, it did show us how fast our men could move in an emergency. On the 29th, after twenty-six days at sea, we landed at Taranto, Italy, all of us extremely happy to set foot once more on solid ground. We didn't stay happy any too long though. In a very short time, we got tired of getting our feet so solidly to the ground. We marched with full pack to our staying area, five miles away from our landing point, the whole distance seemingly uphill.[2]

Likewise, the pilots of the 302nd Fighter Squadron recorded:

After spending about ten days at the staging area at Taranto, the squadron was moved on 7 February by motor transport across the mountains of Italy to Montecorvino Air Base, Italy. Camp was quickly set up and the squadron again proceeded to function as it had before leaving the States. The remainder of the month of February was spent in completing the training for which the squadron was officially activated.[3]

The three squadrons disembarked at the end of January and beginning of February. The first operations were flown around the middle of February and consisted of fleet patrol, convoy escort, reconnaissance and strafing missions. Harbor patrol was important, because the harbor contained a lot of military materiel destined for the front lines, and the patrols prevented the Axis from raiding it.

About this, Lieutenant Colonel Davis remarked:

Soon after landing in Italy […] I was thoroughly disgusted and angered to learn that the 332nd had been assigned to coastal patrol. The assignment was a direct result of the initial Mediterranean theater assessment and the evaluation of the 99th Fighter Squadron's performance during its first three months in the theater, since the G3 reassessment was not completed until March. To assign the group to a noncombat role at a critical juncture in the war seemed a betrayal of everything we had been working for, and an intentional insult to me and my men. I expressed my feelings to no one, however. I had to show to all concerned an attitude that what we were doing was vitally important to the theater mission, whether I believed it or not.

The 332nd was assigned to the 62nd Fighter Wing, 12th Air Force, under the command of Col. Robert Israel. We were to replace the 81st Fighter Group on 15 February, when that group moved out of the theater. Our mission would be convoy escort, harbor protection, scrambles, point patrol, reconnaissance, and strafing.

Harbor and convoy protection were significant missions because of the large quantities of war materiel that were coming in daily for all units in the theater. The protection of convoys traveling from Naples to Anzio, the only line of supply for our forces operating there, was of vital importance. We were to patrol the area from Cape Palenuro and the Gulf of Felicastro to the Ponsiano Islands, assuring our ground forces a continuous flow of supplies.[4]

The feelings that Davis described were also present in the 301st war history. On 18 February, "the squadron wonders how the war is struggling along without them. 'Helped' another convoy."[5] A few days later, on the 22nd, "More convoy protection. Those convoys don't know how lucky they are with the 301st covering them."[6] In March, April, and May the missions mostly have consisted of escorting convoys, escorting shipping in the Tyrrhenian Sea, harbor patrol and strafing. The convoy patrols consisted of providing cover for the patrols that left the Naples Harbor and made their way to the beachhead at Anzio. This was the only supply line to the troops operating there.

Meanwhile, the strafing missions could be very intense. Joseph Gomer recalled about strafing missions:

Ground fire was only on strafing missions. That was the most distasteful of all, because the ground was blinking at you. I had the plane in front of me get hit, the plane behind me get hit. Other than that, all we had to worry about was flak. If the Germans could track you for seventeen seconds, they could put that first burst right up. They were good.[7]

On 3 February, Captain DeBow of the 301st Fighter Squadron needed to go to the hospital and was replaced by Lieutenant Rayford; Captain DeBow returned on the 20th. On the 7th the 301st left camp and went by car to Montecorvino Airdrome, where it would set up camp. The first pilots of the unit took to the air on 15 February.

The 332nd Fighter Group relocated from Montecorvino airfield to Capodichino airfield. Settling in a new place can be challenging and some of the cooks resorted to drinking. This, and carelessness, caused the cooks' tent of the 100th Fighter Squadron to burn down on 17 February. On the 26th, the squadron's history recorded: "The cooks are drunk again. One (Ralph Knights) went to the guard house. Staff Sergeant Charlie Golden is being relieved of his duties as mess sergeant."[8] Sergeant Rufus Higgins, the new mess sergeant, would later be praised for the food that he served the enlisted men.[9]

As the 301st Fighter Squadron history recounted:

> The 23rd was a sad day for us. Four of our pilots were up on a training mission around Avellino when the weather closed in on them. One of them, Lieutenant Ulysses S. Taylor, was forced to bail out in the sea. Luckily, he was picked up by a motor launch, after staying in the water for a little less than an hour, and taken to a hospital where he was treated for shock and exposure. Another, Lieutenant Langston, had quite a bit of difficulty with his plane, going into spin after spin. Finally, he decided to jump, but just when he was about to leave the plane, he spotted the coast line through the soup, righted his plane, and landed at Pompeii, sans door. The third man, Lieutenant Wiggins, managed to get back to the base without a mishap. The fourth man, Lieutenant Harry Daniels, was lost soon after they got into the bad weather, and no trace of either he or his plane has been found since. Lieutenant Daniels was a very likeable fellow, and the entire squadron grieved his loss.[10]

On 24 February, a .50 caliber machine gun went off in one of the planes of the 100th Fighter Squadron. Seventy-two rounds were fired, but no one was injured.

Later that month, on the 27th, Lieutenant Paul F. Byrd of the 301st Fighter Squadron would be confined to the hospital. He had been wounded by an accidental discharge of what was presumed to be an unloaded gun. He would recover, but until that time the squadron had no weather officer. Captain DeBow was relieved of his command of the 301st on 28 February, and First Lieutenant Lee Rayford took over. That same day, a flight on convoy escort spotted a life raft and reported its location.

In the beginning of March, the 301st pilots continued to provide convoy protection and fly training missions. Most of the pilots were eager to get into combat.

The next month changes would arrive, as recounted by Lieutenant Colonel Davis:

> Early in March Gen. Ira Eaker, commander, Mediterranean Allied Air Force, requested that I report to his headquarters at Caserta. He described a plan to transfer the 332nd from its coastal patrol mission to bomber escort with the 306th Wing, 15th Fighter Command. This decision must have been based in part on the G3 reassessment of the 99th's performance, which had just been completed. General Eaker pointed out the contribution the 332nd could make to reducing heavy losses of B-17s and B-24s (the command had lost 114 planes the previous month). Under this plan, we would be reequipped with P-47s and join the escort mission now being performed by the other fighter groups in the 15th Fighter Command. Needless to say, I leaped at the opportunity. The escort mission was vitally important to the war, and our new aircraft would enable us to meet the Germans with the same altitude and speed capability that previously had given them definite advantages over our P-40s.
>
> On 29 May 1944, shortly after the 332nd was transferred to the 306th Wing in Brig. Gen. Dean C. ("Doc") Strother's 15th Fighter Command, I was promoted to colonel. Unlike the 62nd Wing, the 15th Fighter Command (the fighter arm

of the 15th Strategic Air Force) had an offensive mission. Composed of several groups equipped with P-47s, P-51s, and P-38s, the command escorted the heavy bombers of the 15th Air Force—B-17s and B-24s—on their far-ranging missions to the Balkans, Romania, Austria, Czechoslovakia, Germany, France, Spain, Yugoslavia, northern Italy, Bulgaria, and Greece. It was also able to carry out offensive fighter missions, usually strafing attacks on suitable targets in the 15th's area of operations.[11]

Before that happened, in March 1944 the 332nd Fighter Squadron was involved in convoy escort, scrambling for enemy aircraft, harbor protection and air-sea rescue. The rains proved to be a problem for the squadron in March, as is recounted in the 301st Fighter Squadron history: "There is definite hope that the rains may cease. […] Today however is another non-flying day." "Beautiful March weather is still holding out." "Mud as usual and rain. This would be a very 'Merciful' country by the 'Bard of the Avond'." "More rain, more rest."[12]

On 2 March, the 100th squadron history recorded: "Most of the squadron dug slit trenches; same promptly used during firing of AA guns in the early hours of the night. Sergeant Rufus Higgins, our new mess sergeant continues to receive the praise of enlisted men for the fine food that is being served."[13] On 2 March 1944, a plane of the 302nd Fighter Squadron was lost due to a fire after a forced landing. Luckily the pilot was unhurt.

On 6 March, the squadron departed Montecovino air base and went to Capodichino. On the 9th, tragedy struck the squadron once more. Lieutenant Wayne V. Liggins was killed when his plane crashed on a training mission. The squadron felt the losses dearly, as there had been many accidents recently.

On 11 March 1944, Lieutenant Holsclaw of the 100th Fighter Squadron collided with a P-47 parked on the field while landing in the dark, damaging his plane and injuring himself. During a point patrol on 11 March the 302nd Fighter Squadron sighted a dinghy and the occupants were rescued.

On 13 March a hostile aircraft was sighted, by the 302nd Fighter Squadron, but it eluded the pilots.

On 14 March, a flight led by First Lieutenant D.M. Watson, of the 302nd Fighter Squadron, of which a sub-flight of two aircraft was led by Second Lieutenant L.D. Wilkins, encountered a Ju-88 Recce type A-5. The plane was chased for over thirty minutes. Lieutenant Wilkins fired until his ammunition was exhausted. Many pieces broke away from the hostile aircraft. Smoke came from the left engine and the plane lost speed. When the ammunition was exhausted however, Wilkins stopped the chase. The claim was made as enemy aircraft damaged.

The men would soon get some of the excitement that they desired, but not in the sense that they had been looking for. On 15 March, the 100th Fighter Squadron was woken up early. As the squadron's history recorded:

> Jerry started our day for us, coming over around 01:30 hours, he aroused everyone in the squadron. No damage was done to personnel or planes. Frantic digging was observed all during day as officers and enlisted men dug in for any eventuality.[14]

Similarly, the 301st Fighter Squadron history recorded:

> At 03:00 hours on the 15th, enemy aircraft flew over our area. Anti-aircraft guns blasted the peaceful stillness of the night for about fifteen minutes. They told us about it the next morning. We were asleep. Either the squadron was very brave or very tired. In the afternoon of that same day, the squadron had its first scramble. Lieutenants Wiggins and Gomer attempted to intercept a Reconnaissance Plane that was seen flying around over our heads. Interception was not made.[15]

On the 16th, a boogie was chased for twenty miles by the 302nd Fighter Squadron, but it was identified as friendly.

On 17 March, 100th Fighter Squadron recorded:

> What started as a routine day changed. Lieutenant Turner, operations officer, was the laughing stock of the pilots today

when he nosed over his plane on landing. This was his first accident since beginning to fly. Everyone is still waiting for Jerry to visit us again.[16]

The eruption of Mount Vesuvius on 17 March also caused considerable problems for Allied aircraft in the vicinity, which included the 332nd Fighter Group. The rain of cinders and clouds of ash from the eruption caused all flying to cease for a few days. "Now the squadron has seen it all. Today it's raining volcanic ash. Vesuvius is erupting and doing a truly noble job of it. The [301st Fighter Squadron] is awaiting orders to 'Put that volcano out'."[17] The next day:

> Vesuvius is still holding the center of the stage. Ash is about four inches deep. All flying has been suspended. There is much discussion as to how long Vesuvius can hold out at the present rate. Long forgotten science is being recalled. Earthquake and tidal wave possibilities are being discussed.[18]

The eruption of Mount Vesuvius had coated the area with a layer of fine ash. This environmental disaster had lingering effects on the fighter units in the area. On 24 May, when Lieutenant Virgil Richardson became an unwilling butcher when a flock of ash-covered sheep wandered on to the airfield as he tried to land:

> I didn't have much time to react. My nose wheel broke and suddenly I saw parts of dead sheep flying about. Then the gas tank, located directly under my seat, caught fire. Let me tell you, there is nothing that can make you move faster than a having a live fire under your ass! In a flash, I pulled the lever to open my door. To my surprise, the door fell completely off! I quickly unbuckled my seatbelt.[19]

However, the skidding plane veered to the right and threw him to the ground. He landed on his dinghy and it broke his fall. His injuries kept him in bed for several weeks.

As the squadron history recounted,

Swastikas there have been on planes and Rising Suns, but to Lieutenant "M'Lord" Richardson goes the unique distinction of the Lamb Chop. Lieutenant Richardson totally demolished twenty-three sheep who ambled across the runway in his path as he was landing.[20]

Besides the slaughtered sheep, Richardson had also destroyed his plane.

On 18 March, the 100th Fighter Squadron suffered its first casualty overseas. While searching for the wreckage of a JU-88, Lieutenant Clemenceau Givings developed mechanical problems. He bailed out, but became entangled in his parachute and drowned in Naples harbor.

Photograph shows goats on a runway, with airplanes in the background, in Ramitelli, Italy, March 1945. (Courtesy of Library of Congress)

On 20 March the 100th Fighter Squadron received new P-39s; on the 23rd Lieutenant Wilkins, of the 302nd Fighter Squadron, crashed on take-off, but the pilot was unhurt.

On 28 March a flight led by first Lieutenant Roy M. Spencer, of the 302nd Fighter Squadron, was patrolling the island of Panza D'Ischia:

> The two aircraft flown by Lts Spencer and Melton encountered one Ju-88 heading north. A long chase followed at high speed, about 310 mph [500 kph]. The hostile aircraft bobbed between 5 and 50ft above the water and made turns alternately of about 30 degrees. He headed directly into the sun on one leg and northwest on the other. Many .50 cal. tracers were seen to enter the fuselage of the enemy aircraft and the right engine was left smoking. The chase broke off after ammunition of the one plane was expended and the armament electrical system of the other went out.[21]

A claim was made for a damaged aircraft.

On 30 March, a truck was driving away from the camp area. When approaching a railway track, the operator had failed to lower the bars and the vehicle attempted to cross the track. While doing so, it was hit by a locomotive. Both Staff Sergeant Cathedral Smith and Sergeant Jenkins H. Bluitt were injured. Bluitt died the next day as a result of his injuries.

On 31 March, Lieutenant Norvell Stoudmire, of the 100th Fighter Squadron, was flying harbor patrol when his plane suddenly caught fire and he tried to bail out. However, his parachute became entangled in the aircraft and both the pilot and his machine crashed into the sea.

On 2 April, two planes of the 302nd Fighter Squadron crashed upon landing. They landed in the darkness and in intense dust clouds created by previously landed aircraft. The planes were damaged, but the pilots unhurt.

On 4 April, Lieutenant Wilkerson, of the 100th Fighter Squadron, bailed out of his plane while on a training flight and landed in a tree, resulting in a broken leg.

According to the squadron history, 6 April was just a "Routine day. Quite a few men lost their appetites when the discovered beans and macaroni on the menu today."[22]

On 15 April, the 332nd Fighter Group was complete again, when the 301st and the 302nd Fighter Squadron joined the 100th Fighter Squadron at Capodichino. This new airfield had a number of luxuries that were lacking in the other airbase – an electrical generator for one thing.

On 16 April, Lieutenant Westmoreland of the 302nd Fighter Squadron bailed out of his aircraft after exhausting his fuel supply and suffered an injured ankle. Lieutenants Bussy and Hunter made forced landings at Largo airbase at Castel Volturno.

On 17 April ,1944, Lieutenant Wyatt crashed while on a routine point patrol. He sustained serious injuries and died two days later during the morning; he was buried that same afternoon.

On 18 April, Conner Wilson, supply officer in the 301st Fighter Squadron, was making a trip to Bari when the truck he was travelling went out of control and over an embankment. He tried to bail out, but was injured, and the driver sustained a scratched face.

On 22 April, 1944, Lieutenant Edward Gleed was assigned to the 301st Fighter Squadron, while the Lieutenant Melvin T. Jackson was

Lieutenant Edward C. Gleed is explaining to the pilots of the Fighter Group that day's mission. (Courtesy of National Archives and Records Administration)

moved from the 100th Fighter Squadron to the 302nd to take over as squadron commander.

While taking off for a pre-dawn strafing mission on 24 April, Second Lieutenant Edgar Jones of the 100th Fighter Squadron lost control over his P-39 and crashed into a parked plane. He died in the crash. There was an air raid that same day and many of the men returned to their tent to find bits of shrapnel that had fallen during their absence; there were no casualties. The next day the first P-47s arrived. Six of them had arrived as second-hand from the 325th Fighter Group.

On 4 May 1944, the 302nd Fighter Squadron was engaged in a strafing patrol covering twenty-two miles of road between Sora and Avezzano. Twelve airplanes took off, departing at 13:00 hours. Hostile trucks were spotted and engaged; the fighters were also fired upon by inaccurate and ineffective anti-aircraft artillery. They landed again at 14:50 hours.

On 5 May, First Lieutenant James Polkinghorne of the 301st Fighter Squadron went missing on a strafing mission near Terracina, on the Italian west coast. There were thick clouds over the target, but when a small opening was located two flights descended. However, the clouds kept obscuring the target and the two flights ascended again, while being fired upon by the enemy. When returning to base it became obvious that Polkinghorne was missing; neither his body nor his plane were ever recovered.

That same day transitional flights in the P-47 were made by pilots of the 100th Fighter Squadron. The 302nd likewise started transitional flights in May. Several enlisted men of the 302nd Fighter Squadron were assigned to the 325th Fighter Group to acquire experience in working with the P-47. Just like the pilots, they, too, needed to gain familiarity with the aircraft.

On 13 May, Henry Pollard, a former member of the famous "Jimmie Lunceford Orchestra", was assigned to the 302nd Fighter Squadron.

On 13, 17, 21 and 27 May, the pilots of the 100th provided cover for naval vessels that were shelling hostile shores.

On 14 May, Lieutenant Commie Wilson, supply officer with 301st Fighter Squadron, was cleaning a hat in his tent when he was severely burned by a gasoline fire. His hands and his face severely suffered and he was confined to hospital.

On 15 May, Lieutenant Joe P. Gomer, 301st Fighter Squadron, became a bogey for a while. At a nearby airfield, the planes scrambled when they spotted a P-47 in the air and assumed it was a hostile "bogey". Gomer, the "bogey", returned to the airfield unaware of his new found status.[23]

On 16 May, 1944 Lieutenant Laird, 100th Fighter Squadron, did not lower his landing gear and damaged his plane in a belly landing.

On 18 May, the 302nd provided cover for a convoy named "brunette" during intense coastal shelling operations in support of the 5th Army and its advance to Gaeta, a city about halfway between the landing sites at Anzio and Naples. No hostile aircraft were encountered.

In the afternoon of 19 May, 1st Lieutenant Dudly M. Watson and Second Lieutenant J.J. Suggs, of the 302nd Fighter Squadron, scrambled to search for a bandits approximately twelve miles north-north-east of the base. They were then vectored to another place. Once there, the two pilots saw a bomber crew in the water. Immediately relief was called and cover was provided until the air sea rescue was complete.

On the same day, during a transition flight with a P-47, Second Lieutenant Othel Dickson, of the 301st Fighter Squadron, suffered an engine failure. He totally wrecked the plane during a belly landing and earned the nickname "Iron Pants" after he walked away from it.

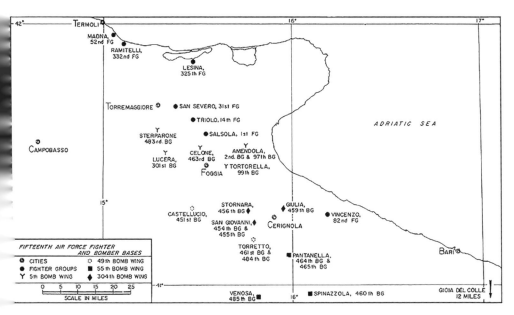

A map of all the bomber groups and fighter groups in the Fifteenth Air Force. (Public Domain)

On 22 May 1944, the 332nd Fighter Group was transferred from the 12th Air Force to the 15th Air Force. The advance detachments departed a few days later for Ramitelli airfield, to be joined by the rest of the fighter group soon afterwards. The unit was removed from coastal patrol missions and added to the bomber escorts. The missions would be fought over German territory.

That same day, Henry Pollard, of the 302nd Fighter Squadron, died when his airplane crashed and caught fire during a forced landing. Pollard was trapped in his cockpit and couldn't escape in time. He had been with the squadron less than ten days.

On 23 May, Lieutenant Dickson of 100th Fighter Squadron made a forced landing at Castel Volturno, after his plane had engine trouble. On 24 May John Prowell Jr., of the 301st Fighter Squadron, was killed when he crashed while protecting a convoy. A day later, 25 May, Lieutenant Sherard, of the 100th Fighter Squadron, made a forced landing on the Anzio beachhead. As Lieutenant Earl S. Sherard recounted of the event:

> While on convoy patrol our controller vectored the flight, led by Lieutenant W.W. Crockett, to Anzio beachhead. After being in position for about an hour, my ships belly tank broke loose and fouled the main fuel line, causing the engine to start cutting out. I informed Lieutenant Crockett of the trouble and began to head for land. Just off shore the engine cut out completely on all tanks. At the same time, I spotted the landing strip that was located on the beach head, and made a wheels-down landing on the strip. I was given excellent cover at all times by Lieutenant Crockett. After my plane had been serviced and I had started to return to my home base, several army officers rushed up to me and asked me to do them a favor. Naturally, I said I would. They informed me that they had the first pictures of the history-making meeting between the Allied forces, making Anzio no longer a beachhead. They asked me to carry the pictures back to army special services officer, located near our field, saying that I would be doing the people at home a great favor by furnishing first hand pictures that otherwise might be delayed indefinitely.[24]

On the 24th, Lieutenant John Prowell, of the 301st Fighter Squadron, went missing during a routine convoy escort mission. He had developed engine trouble and bailed out. Air sea rescue managed to find his dinghy, but did not locate him. He was eventually declared dead.

On the 25th, the advance echelon of the 301st Fighter Squadron, left Montecorvino airfield to go to Ramitelli, where they would set up. The rest of the squadron joined them on the 30th.

On 28 May, Lieutenant Brown, of the 100th Fighter Squadron, ditched his plane in a harbor after it had developed engine trouble.

On 29 May 1944, Benjamin Davis, commanding officer of the 332nd Fighter Group, was promoted to colonel. That same day, Lieutenant Lloyd S. Hathcock, of the 301st went missing while ferrying a plane from Montecorvino to Ramitelli. "It is believed he slightly overshot and landed in enemy territory."[25] He had become disorientated during the flight and had landed at an airfield still held by the Germans, who took him prisoner and captured his Thunderbolt intact.

The aircraft was taken for evaluation to the Rechlin Test Center and was later transferred to the Zirkus Rosarius, a specialist test squadron of the Luftwaffe, where it was used to familiarize the Luftwaffe pilots with Allied planes through mock combat.

Through this, the German pilots and engineers could learn the weaknesses and the strengths of the planes. Hathcock's Thunderbolt was the first intact P-47 to be captured. It was found near the end of the war at the Göttingen airfield, when the base was overrun by American troops.

On 1 June the 302nd Fighter Squadron moved to Ramitelli air base. As the squadron's war diary recounted:

> The new surroundings proved quite different from the hustle and bustle of the Naples area. Many were griping over the changed conditions, but none could deny that the present location is much more conductive to efficient operation. The pilots of the squadron were still engaged in transition training in the P-47 type aircraft.[26]

At Ramitelli, the airbase was close to the beach and everyone benefited from this.

On 2 June, Master Sergeant William Harris, of the 302nd Fighter Squadron, was killed when the truck he was travelling in was struck by an aircraft which was taking off on a local flight. That same day Second Lieutenant Elmer Taylor, of the 302nd Fighter Squadron, died when his aircraft crashed into the ground during a training flight. He was unable to bail out.

Between 6 and 10 June the 100th Fighter Squadron was transported to the Ramitelli airfield in four parts. Escorting bombers became the most important missions for the rest of the month.

On 6 June, D-Day in Normandy, the advance echelon of the 100th Fighter Squadron left Capodichino for Ramitelli airfield. The next day the second group of the 100th Fighter Squadron departed. Thieves made use of the darkness of the night to steal clothing and equipment. The third group arrived on 9 June, except for a truck which had turned

Sergeant William P. Bostic, 301st Fighter Squadron, in control tower in Ramitelli, Italy, March 1945. (Courtesy of Library of Congress)

The control tower is essential for the operations of a Fighter Group. (Courtesy of National Archives and Records Administration)

over – Sergeant John R. Perry suffered a broken leg, but the driver was unhurt. On 10 June the last group arrived. The planes also arrived, under command of Captain Tresville.

On 7 June, 32 P-47s performed a fighter sweep over the area of Ferrara-Bologna. They found little activity other than a small amount of flak. On the way to the target area, Second Lieutenant Carroll Langston Jr. noticed that he was losing oil pressure and he jumped out of his plane. However, his parachute caught on his plane and he was unable to get loose in time. His body was found nineteen days later when it washed ashore. Several other pilots had the same problem, saying that their oil pressure was low, and the ground crews repaired this.

On 8 June, the 332nd took off with thirty-two planes to escort the 5th Bombardment Wing B-17 to the north of Italy, then the city of Pola, to bomb targets. The events over Pola were uneventful. Colonel Davis had stressed that the pilots must protect the bombers. Other fighters might engage targets of opportunity, but the pilots of the 332nd had to stay with the bombers. Twelve or sixteen planes would fly over the bombers to provide cover.

On 9 June, however, things were different. Thirty-nine P-47s took off, from the 301st and the 302nd Fighter Squadron and they linked up with bombers of the 5th, 49th, 55th, 57th and 304th Bombardment Wings. Their target: Munich. As Benjamin O. Davis wrote about the mission:

> Our third P-47 mission was penetration escort for B-17s and B-24s to the heavily defended Munich area. As the formation leader I was responsible for the takeoff from Ramitelli and joining up in a way that would enable us to rendezvous with the bombers. We had to position ourselves carefully so that we could react to the radio calls announcing the presence and location of enemy fighters. We also had to accommodate the bombers: sometimes they were early, sometimes late; sometimes they changed direction and altitude because of cloud cover. The B-17s usually flew higher than the B-24s, but we had to maintain an altitude that would enable us to take care of the entire force. Bombers dropping to the rear of the formation because of battle damage were also our responsibility. Our pilots had to stay in a position to attack enemy fighters as they made their passes at the friendly formations, and they had to protect our own formation at the same time, so our eyes had to be everywhere. As we approached Munich, I dispatched Capt. Red Jackson's 302d Squadron to meet a threat developing at the high right rear side. Simultaneously, two Me-109s flew through the squadron I was leading. We took our best possible defensive maneuver, turning into them. In the turn, I fired a wide deflection shot at the closest enemy fighter without visible results. Captain Jackson gave this report in his debriefing: "An Me-109 came in on my tail … out of the clouds behind me; a dogfight ensued until I shot the Me-109 down. Metal flew off his left side as the door flew off. The Nazi pilot bailed out over a German airfield. I hit the deck and came home. Flak was everywhere." Including Captain Jackson's kill, we destroyed a total of five enemy fighters. Over the Udine area enemy fighters attacked

the B-24s, and we were able to damage one Me-109. Upon our return to Ramitelli we received the following message from one of the bombardment wing commanders: "Your formation flying and escort work is the best we have ever seen."[27]

During the escort mission, however, Cornelius Rogers developed engine trouble and went missing.

At the camp, Staff Sergeant Samuel Jacobs, the crew chief of Wendell O. Pruitt, was receiving instructions about the P-47. Pruitt, as well as Lee Archer, was one of the pilots that had shot down a German airplane. As Jacobs recalled:

> We had been flying Thunderbolts for about a week. Some representatives from Republic Aviation, and some Air Corps brass had been scheduled to arrive and teach us how to fly, and crew the 47s. However, by the time they arrived, our Engineering Officers and Line Chiefs had schooled us on everything we needed to know, and we'd already flown a couple of missions. I remember this major standing atop a munition's carrier telling us "Boys" all about the " flying bathtub" and how it should never be slow rolled below a thousand feet, due to its excessive weight. No sooner had he finished his statement than "A" flight was returning from its victorious mission. Down on the deck, props cutting grass, came Lieutenants Pruitt and his wingman Lee Archer, nearly touching wings. Lieutenant Pruitt pulled up into the prettiest victory roll you'd ever see, with Archer right in his pocket, as the major screamed, "YOU CAN'T DO THAT!!!!"[28]

On 11 June, thirty aircraft from the 301st and 302nd Fighter Squadron provided escort for the bombers of the 5th and the 55th Bombardment Wing. The target was Smederevo, in Yugoslavia. On the 13th the same two squadrons flew escorts for the 5th and 49th Bombardment Wing when they attacked Munich. Although eleven of the Luftwaffe were seen, only four pressed home their attack.

On 14 June, a mission was sent to Budapest, Hungary. The 301st and the 302nd put twenty-nine planes in the air to escort the 5th, 49th, 55th, 304th

Bombardment Wing. Fifteen Me-109s and seven twin-engine fighters were seen, they did not attempt to engage the fighters and the bombers.

On 14 June, Roger B. Brown, 100th Fighter Squadron, went missing during a training flight. His plane developed engine trouble and crashed. Since it was unclear if he managed to bail out or not, Brown was initially listed as missing. In September, however, his family received word that Brown had died in the crash.

On 16 June, forty P-47s went to Bratislava, where the 100th, 301st, 302nd provided escort for bombers. The mission was uneventful. That same day, eight pilots of the 100th Fighter Squadron went on a mission to Hungary. Nine pilots left for Algiers in the morning to ferry back new planes. On 19 June four pilots returned with new planes.

On the 20th, a strafing mission took off, but failed to reach the target in the bad weather.

On 22 June, forty-one planes from the 332nd took off on a strafing mission on the Airasca-Pinerolo airbase in north-west Italy. Only thirty-six got there. Four planes needed to return due to mechanical issues, while Gwynne Peirson had crashed on takeoff – thankfully, surviving.

To take the airfield by surprise, the aircraft were to fly low over the water. Just off the coast, Charles Johnson got too low, touched the water and exploded on impact. Earl Sherard's P-47 also hit the water, though he managed to get out. Samuel Jefferson, circling Sherard's machine, touched the water with his aircraft and sank to the bottom before he could escape.

Tresvile, the 100th Fighter Squadron commander, also died when his plane struck the water. The propeller was bent over the cowling, the drop tanks ripped off and the ailerons. The radio silence prevented the deputy formation leader from taking over, as he never knew of the loss.

Henry Scott recalled Captain Tresville's last flight:

> It was horrible. I was flying in the same flight with the captain. We had strafed everything we could find when the group leader's plane was hit. [This is the plane flown by Tresville.] We were flying as close to the ground as we could get – he didn't have a chance. His plane hit the ground and exploded almost immediately and I had to look at him sitting in the cockpit. It was terrible.[29]

Andrew Turner took over command of the 100th Fighter Squadron.

On 23 June, the 332nd provided escort for bombers attacking Bucharest Giurgiu in Romania. No enemies were encountered. On 25 June, fighters of the 100th, 301st, and the 302nd took off in flights of four. Their task was to perform strafing missions in the north of Italy to prevent the enemy from bringing up supplies successfully. Wendell O. Pruitt, Gwynne W. Peirson, Freddie Hutchins and Larry Wilkins, all of the 302nd Fighter Squadron, took off together.

A Tuskegee Airmen together with two Italian children. (Courtesy of Craig Huntly)

Hutchins and Wilkins returned early when Hutchins was incapable of fulfilling the mission. Pruitt and Peirson continued the mission together. However, they never found their target, but on their way back they came across the harbor of Trieste and saw a ship they identified as a German destroyer - the black cross was clearly visible on the funnel. The two men moved to engage and soon set the boat on fire. The vessel was the former Italian destroyer TA-22, now being used as a mine-laying torpedo-boat by the Germans. The smoke attracted other pilots and another flight joined in: Joseph Elsberry, Joseph Lewis, Henry B. Scott, and Charles Dunne, all of the 301st Fighter Squadron.

When Peirson made another pass, his rounds struck one of the mines on board the ship and it exploded. Once the air was clear again, the pilots could see the ship was rolling over and sinking. The group then engaged radar installations and radio stations around the harbor, attacked the wharf at Muggio, and sank a sailing boat which fired at them. Peirson's plane had several holes on the underside of his wings, probably from the debris of the explosion.

Lieutenant Henry B. Scott recounted his experiences:

> There were six fliers in our small group, Lieutenant Joseph Elsberry, Lieutenant Gwynne Peirson, Lieutenant Charles Dunne, Lieutenant Joe Lewis, Lieutenant Wendell Pruitt, and myself. We were returning to our base after completing our mission, still looking for targets of opportunity. Then we saw this baby steaming around. We were flying only about 10 or 15ft above the water at the time. The ship wasn't attacked when we first sighted it because we didn't know whether it was Allied or not, but when it didn't display the colors of the day we began to let go with everything we had.
>
> The flak was so thick when that destroyer opened up that it looked like a blanket. It was throwing everything it had at us and at 9 o'clock in the morning it was so dark you'd think it was midnight. That was just how thick the flak was.
>
> Our squadron leader, Lieutenant Elsberry, went in first. I was the second to make a pass. We gave it a good blasting from front to rear. Charles Dunne, the third man to attack, told me later he saw smoke and fire begin to pour out over

mid-ship after I had gone over. I can't definitely say that it was my gunfire that started this destruction and I won't. But I know I did get in some good bursts.

Gwynne Peirson, the last man to get in a lick, really gave that tin can a pasting, because when we made the second pass it was really burning. Elsberry went over last the second time and just as he got in for number two the whole damned thing blew right out of the water. We don't know till yet what the ship was carrying, but I think it must have been land mines or some high explosives to blow up the way it did. Seeing that baby blow up was the greatest thrill I ever had in my life.[30]

On 26 June, thirty-six Thunderbolts took to the air to escort bombers to the Lake Balaton area. Two of the pilots needed to bail out after they got problems with their planes. Andrew Maples jumped out near Termoli and was later returned to the fighter group. Maurice Esters was less lucky, being forced out of his plane over the Adriatic Sea after his plane developed engine failure. As Luther Smith recalled: "He was on his raft and waved to us that he was all right moments before a huge wave swept him under. We never saw him again."[31] Esters was declared dead on 27 June 1945. Also on the 26th, the first P-51s arrived at Ramitelli, ferried in by two pilots of the 100th Fighter Squadron. The pilots were eager to try out their new machines and transitional flights would start soon after.

On 27 June, thirty-seven Thunderbolts escorted bombers to Budapest. The 5th Bombardment Wing and the 47th Bombardment Wing needed and escort and thirty-seven P-47s took off to provide escort for them. Larry Wilkins and Washington Ross damaged their planes after landing in an accident.

On 28th June, the pilots started transitioning to North American P-51s, also known as Mustangs. The P-51 had its first flight in October 1940, and the P-51D had a bubble canopy, which had the benefit of allowing greater visibility. Armed with six machine guns, it could put out a lethal amount of firepower. The pilots hoped that soon more of the enemy would be encountered – and that Christmas could be celebrated at home again. That same day, the 304th Bombardment Wing needed an escort and thirty-seven planes took to the skies. Edward Laird was killed when his aircraft left the runway while taking off; Lieutenant Mac Ross performed an emergency landing at Lecce airfield; Alfonza Davis' P-47 blew a tire during taking off and made a landing at Otranto when the mission was over. Lieutenant Floyd Thompson was taken prisoner after he jumped out of his plane near Forli.

On 30 June, forty-five aircraft of the 100th, 301st, 302nd took off; two planes returned due to mechanical problems. Five bombardment wings attacked the Munich area. It would be the last mission flown in the P-47. New bubbletop P-47s had arrived, but the 332nd Fighter Group transitioned to the P-51s. These were second-hands from the 31st and 325th Fighter Group. The Thunderbolts of the 332nd were passed along to the 86th Fighter Group.[32]

Combat rotation

Combat rotation was employed by the USAAF during the Second World War. This was done primarily for two reasons: first, combat is mentally and physically tiring and can result in a multitude of disorders, both physical and mental. The idea of rotation was to allow combat-weary crews and pilots a chance to rest, while at the same time, the combat veterans could share their latest experiences with new cadets and help develop better aircraft and materiel.[33]

Second, employing combat weary crew also posed a risk, both to themselves and their fellow pilots. Likewise, pilots pushed beyond their breaking point needed a long time to recover, if they ever recovered at all. Shorter periods of leave might allow a pilot to serve in combat longer, but they could not serve indefinitely. Additional pilots were also needed to replace those lost due to accident or disease.

In the case of the 332nd Fighter Group, this posed a problem. Because it was a segregated unit, only Black Americans could serve in it, meaning it was entirely dependent on how many Black pilots could be trained at the limited facilities in the USA. With the establishment of the 477th Bombardment Group, a segregated bombardment group, pilots were needed for both units, but the options were limited. As a result, Black pilots serving in the 332nd Fighter Group might fly longer than their white counterparts.

Furthermore, the newly arrived pilots needed to be integrated into the unit. The new pilots were inexperienced. No matter how many hours they had trained, real missions were always different than the simulated ones. As Harold Brown, who had earned his wings on 23 May 1944, described his first mission:

> There's a reasonable amount of apprehension. Here's where it now starts settling in. Before it was all fun and games. Now you're going off on a real mission. First thing you sweated out was that little single engine. Is this engine going to run for the six hours the way it was advertised? Get you there and get you home. Because there were many guys who flew missions, engine trouble and whatnot, and wound up either jumping out, bailing out or crash landing strictly because of engine problems. Not a bullet had touched them. But they still parked it up in Germany someplace or if they were able to get it back over the bomb line up in northern Italy then they parked it there.
>
> So first you always sweated out the engine. Other than that, on that first mission apprehensions came from I wonder if we're going to run into any fighters or if we're going to run into anything. Well, it was uneventful. We picked up our bombers, flew a fairly normal mission, didn't encounter any enemy fighters, nothing. Very routine. Nothing but just a long mission. About six, six and a half hours long. By the time you got back you were tired. Sitting in that little cramped cockpit and boom, that was the first mission. But you're happy to get it over with.[34]

The Luftwaffe in 1944

Vastly outnumbered in fighters and bombers, Germany focused technological innovations to turn the tide. One such was the development of the first fighter jets, as the Me-262 and Me-163. The Messerschmitt 262 had its first flight in April 1941. Although impressive and a formidable foe, these planes were too few in number to make a difference in the outcome of the war.

Furthermore, the effects of the bombing campaigns on the Luftwaffe were beginning to be felt. Starved of natural oil, synthetic oil was used.

However, even supplies of this were inadequate and pilot training was cut as a result.

Long-range Allied fighters further wore down the defensive capabilities of the German Reich. Shortages of fuel and trained pilots had an effect on the Luftwaffe. "In January 1944 Germany was producing 159,000 tons of synthetic fuel a month; by December of that year production was down to 26,000 tons."[35] Overwhelming air superiority prevented the Luftwaffe from raising little more than a token resistance.

Crew rotation was important, because it prevented combat fatigue. In the First World War, combat fatigue had been known as shell shock, and could lead to what we now refer to as post-traumatic stress disorder. To prevent this, crews in the AAF were rotated to the US, allowing them some time to rest and recover from the stresses they had endured. Combat pilots could be employed as trainers or volunteer for a second tour of duty. Meanwhile, there was no rest for the German pilots who continued to fly until they were injured or killed.

While the south of Italy aligned itself with the Allied forces after the surrender, in the north the *Repubblica Sociale Italiana*, the Italian Social Republic, was established. There the *Aeronautica Nazionale Repubblicana*, National Republican Air Force (ANR) was formed. These pilots worked closely with the German Luftwaffe and frequently engaged Allied bombers and fighters. These units employed their own Italian aircraft as well as operating German planes.

Their primary task was intercepting Allied bombers en route to Germany and protecting industrial areas.

The 99th joins the 332nd Fighter Group

The 99th Fighter Squadron was moved from Pignataro, Ciampo field to Orbetello. On 3 July the squadron received orders to join the 332nd Fighter Group at Ramitelli. The unit consisted of the 100th Fighter Squadron, the 301st Fighter Squadron and the 302nd Fighter Squadron. These four squadrons served as the 332nd Fighter Group. The squadron moved to Ramitelli airfield on 28 June, where it joined the 332nd Fighter Group.

The decision to move the 99th to the 332nd was not perceived as a positive one. The 99th pilots viewed the group as inexperienced, while others saw it as a step towards segregation. They were now in an all-Black fighter group, instead of being a component of a white group. The 332nd Fighter Group men were not so happy about the 99th pilots, because they feared that the leadership roles would be assigned to men of the 99th. However, this did not happen.

The unit was a four-squadron group, which did not happen very often. The training meanwhile lagged behind. The Tuskegee Army Air Field needed to train pilots for the 99th Fighter Squadron, 100th Fighter Squadron, 301st Fighter Squadron, 302nd Fighter Squadron, as well as

Several pilots are listening to instructions. (Courtesy of Library of Congress)

the 477th Medium Bombardment Group. This was a bomber group made up of only Black American pilots; as mentioned previously, because the pilots needed to remain longer they had to do more missions than white pilots before they could return to the United States.

In July, the 332nd had changed to the P-51 Mustangs, which were suited for long-range escort missions. The tails of the Mustangs were painted a bright red, and they raised the morale of the group. There were still some tragic incidents however; Othell Dickson was killed when his plane crashed while performing aerobatics, the most likely cause was thought to be the fuselage fuel tank changing the plane's center of gravity

Charles DeBow was relieved as a squadron commander of the 301st and replaced with Lee Rayford of the 99th, who had returned for a second tour of combat. According to Davis, DeBow could not fulfill the position satisfactorily. Mac Ross was also relieved as the squadron's operations officer.

On 4 July 1944, the first mission in the Mustang was made by the 332nd. It escorted the 5th Bombardment Wing and the 47th Bombardment

A crew chief sits on the wing of a P-51 Mustang while the pilot taxies out to take-off. (Courtesy of National Archives and Records Administration)

Staff Sergeant James E. Johnson, head of the sheet metal section of the Fighter Group, spends his spare time painting names on the P-51 Mustangs. (Courtesy of National Archives and Records Administration)

Wing. Forty airplanes soared through the skies to help them. Davis took off with the rest, but returned when his radio had problems.

The next day the 100th, 301st, 302nd provided escort and fifty-two planes took to the skies. Four of the planes lacked enough fuel to return and landed on Corsica. The group saw two Me-109s, but they did not press home their attack.

On 6 July, thirty-seven P-51s escorted the 47th Bombardment Wing to a target; on the 7th, forty-seven P-51s escorted a mission on Vienna.

On the 8th, the 99th worked hard to transition to the P-51s. The same day also saw the 100th, 301st, 302nd in combat, when forty-six Mustangs escorted bombers of the 304th Bombardment Wing to Munchendorf. The attack drew out fifteen to twenty enemy fighters. These were engaged by a group of P-38 Lightnings. One Me-109 made it past the P-38s and attacked Earl Sherard over the target area. Sherard pushed his machine hard to shake off the Me-109, finally losing him. Immediately afterwards however, Sherard was attacked by the P-38s, who thought he was the enemy. After shaking off the Lightnings, an exhausted Sherard landed at a forward airfield.

On 9 July, thirty-two P-51s from the 100th, 301st, 302nd escorted the 47th to the Ploesti region in Romania, a destination where they would be more often. The idea was to starve the German war machine of much needed fuel. Two Me-109s and two FW-190s were seen, but rapidly engaged by other fighters.

Staff Sergeant Alfred D. Norris, crew chief, closes the canopy of a P-51 Mustang for his pilot, Capt. William T. Mattison. (Courtesy of National Archives and Records Administration)

The next two days there were two important casualties. On the 10th, Mac Ross' was killed when his plane went into a shallow dive and struck the side of a hill. There was speculation about suicide, but it was more likely to have been a failing oxygen system.

On the 11th, Captain Leon Roberts, the last member of the original 99th Fighter Squadron to still be with the unit, was killed when his plane crashed into the sea; he, too, was most likely was the victim of a failing oxygen system.

Meanwhile, the date for Operation Dragoon was coming up – landings in the south of France. Several Allied divisions would be put ashore on 15 August 1944 to alleviate pressure on the front at Normandy. Furthermore, harbors in Southern France could be used to deliver supplies to the front.

On 11 July, 100th, 301st, the 302nd escorted with thirty-three P-51s the 47th Bombardment Wing to the submarine pens at Toulon. On 12 July the 49th Bombardment Wing was escorted by the 302nd, while attacking

P-51 Mustangs of the 332nd Fighter Group warming up on the line prior to taking off for escort of heavy bombers en route to enemy targets. Note: the runway is built of interlocking steel matting. (Courtesy of National Archives and Records Administration)

a railway marshalling yard in southern France. Twenty-five German fighters attacked escorts and fierce combat erupted. Joseph Elsberry claimed three kills and got a probable. The unconfirmed kill deprived him of his status as an ace, which he would have been after shooting down five enemy aircraft. It was the last time he saw the enemy up close.

Elsberry saw an FW-190 attack the bombers. He fired on him with a 30-degree deflection shot and the FW-190 fell away. The second FW-190 turned in front of him and he dove slightly to close in on the fighter and engage it. He shot the left wing and the fighter entered a slow roll. The third FW-190 was engaged as Elsberry climbed to go back into the fight. He fired and shots entered the target. The plane crashed into the ground, as seen by Dunne and Friend. Elsberry hit another FW-190 that shot by him. Only the left-wing machine guns were still firing and Elsberry pushed hard to keep the guns on his target. The FW-190 started to spiral down, then dived before crashing into the ground.

Harold Sawyer shot down a plane over Nimes. Six German fighters made a pass at the bombers, diving through the formation. As the fighters escaped, Sawyer fired after them. One of the fighters never recovered and struck the ground. The second FW-190 was fired upon by Sawyer, but this kill was unconfirmed. George Rhodes was shot down and bailed out near Viterbo. He was rescued and returned to the squadron.

On 13 July, the 110th, 301st, 302nd put thirty-seven P-51s in the air to escort two groups of bombers from the 5th Bombardment Wing to the Pinzano railway bridge and the Vinzone viaduct.

On 15 July, the 99th flew for the first time with the other squadrons of the 332nd Fighter Group. The target was the oil refineries at Ploesti. The 55th Bombardment Wing received an escort of sixty-one P-51s. The fighters chased off eight Me-109s which were harassing three straggling bombers near Krusevac. Colonel Davis had stressed that the mission of the fighters was to protect the bombers at all costs.

On 16 July, the 100th, 301st, 302nd performed a fighter sweep over Vienna. A single Macchi C.205 was spotted trying to engage a straggling B-24. Alfonza Davis of the 302nd ordered his flight of four Mustangs to engage the Macchi. They dived on the fighter, but Davis overshot and his wingman, William Green, got inside of the Macchi's turn and fired upon it. The Italian fighter streamed down with black smoke. Green stuck with his target and just before it hit the deck, the Macchi pilot tried

Pilots attend a briefing. (Courtesy of Library of Congress)

to make a turn around a mountain. A wingtip struck the mountain and the plane cartwheeled into a fireball.

Davis was covering Green and he saw a second Macchi far below him. He dived upon this Italian fighter and fired on it, blowing chunks of the fuselage. The Macchi fell to the ground and crashed.

On 17 July, the group provided escort to the 306th Bombardment Wing which attacked the railway marshalling yards at Avignon, and a railway bridge in southern France. The Mustang pilots engaged nineteen Me-109s. Just three pressed home their attack, but they came to regret their decision. The three broke off their attack when they saw the P-51s moving to engage, but were shot down by Luther Smith, Robert Smith and Larry Wilkins.

Maceo Harris was in the same flight and came across a lone, damaged bomber. He escorted it back to Corsica, where both planes landed. The bomber crew was very grateful for the help he had given them.

Walter Palmer missed the rendezvous with his group and decided to set off after them on his own. He hoped to catch up with them. While going there, he encountered a plane that rocked its wings and headed in the opposite direction. This aircraft tried to slip behind him, instead of beside him. The plane was actually a German Me-109 instead of a Mustang. When the German realized that the Palmer was getting into a firing position, the German headed home, while Palmer did likewise.

On 18 July, Lee Rayford led sixty-six Mustangs from the entire group to link up with the bombers en route to the target. They did not find them however, and the group proceeded to fly over the Udine-Treviso area, which was known as an area where the Luftwaffe was active. The target of the bombers was the Luftwaffe base at Memmingen.

Once the bombers approached, the fighters spotted a group of thirty to thirty-five Me-109s approaching the heavy airplanes. The target was then sighted, as well as thirty to forty hostile aircraft. This were mostly Me-109s, FW-190s and Me-410. Four of the FW-190s were moving in for the kill, but were struck down in return.

That day, Clarence Lester shot down three planes. Jack Holsclaw shot down two, and Lee Archer, Charles Bailey, Hugh Warner, Roger Romine, Edward Toppins, Walter Palmer shot down one each. The day was not without loss, however. Lieutenant Gene Browne became a prisoner of war and Lieutenant Wellington G. Irving was killed. Oscar Hutton was lost when his plane was hit by the drop tank of another P-51. Toppins' plane was scrapped due to the fuselage being warped by the speed with which he dove at his enemy.

On 19 July, forty-eight airplanes escorted the 49th BW when the latter attacked Munich/Schleissheim airfield.

On 20 July, the group escorted the 47th 55th and 304th BW to Friedrichshafen and afterwards allowing them a fighter sweep to the northeast of the area. A group of twenty hostile fighters engaged the bombers over the area of Udine. The Luftwaffe tried to lure away the fighters protecting the bombers, by placing groups of four fighters as decoys in the area. The fighters that attacked the bombers were engaged by Joseph Elsberry, Ed Toppins, Langdon Johnson and Armour

Captain Andrew D. Turner and Lieutenant Clarence "Lucky" Lester discuss a recent mission. (Courtesy of National Archives and Records Administration)

McDaniel. They shot down an aircraft each. Two of the bombers were shot down. Lieutenant Perry had a German aircraft in his sights, but his guns jammed. Two air-sea rescue missions were also flown by the 332nd Fighter Group over the Adriatic Sea. During one of the missions the two fighters served as escorts for crippled bombers, guiding them back towards the Italian coast.

On 21 July, the 332nd Fighter Group put sixty aircraft to the skies to link up with the 5th BW when they returned from bombing the Brux synthetic oil refinery. However, the weather prevented the fighters from linking up successfully. Lieutenant William Williams, of the 301st, was reported as lost in the thick clouds. He is still listed as missing in action.

On 22 July, the oil refineries in Ploesti were bombed again. The 332nd Fighter Group escorted the 55th BW. Sixty fighters saw the sixteen to twenty German aircraft, but they were not engaged. James Walker and his flight were escorting a damaged bomber back when they were engaged by German flak. The Mustangs were all damaged and Walker bailed out over Serbia. He evaded captivity and returned to the unit on 28 August 1944.

As Milton Brooks recounted:

> returning to base after leaving the target area, five airplanes, Lt. Walker in the lead ship, were shot at by flak in Yugoslavia. I was flying to the right of Lt Walker's plane and my ship was hit, but not enough to impair flight. Lt. Walker called me and said he was hit and would have to bail out. I didn't see him immediately as the formation broke up but finally located him in a glide about 5,000ft below me with his plane steaming a wide white trail. I circled over him losing altitude along with the other ships. He barely cleared a mountain and the last I saw of him he was right over a little town. I lost sight of him and not seeing any fire or smoke I caught up with another ship and returned to base.[36]

On 24 July 35 P-51s took off and escorted the 47th BG to the harbor at Genoa.

On 25 July, forty-six P-51s escorted the 55th BW in their raid on a tank factory in Linz, Austria. During this mission, the planes formed into three groups, escorting the front, center or rear of the formation. Forty Me-109s attacked the last two groups of eight planes each. In the fight, Harold Sawyer shot down a hostile fighter and damaged two others. Starling Penn and Alfred Carroll were taken prisoner after their planes were shot down.

Staff Sergeant Conige C. Mormon, a crew chief, cleans the glass of Clarence "Lucky" Lester's P-51 Mustang. (Courtesy of National Archives and Records Administration)

On 26 July, sixty-one P-51s took off, but only forty could continue with the mission. The 47th BW needed to be escorted to Vienna, Austria. Two groups of six Me-109s were sighted on their way to the target as well as a group of FW-190s. However, they did not engage the bombers.

Eighteen Me-109s attacked the 332nd, while ten enemy fighters remained high above them to provide cover. Those higher up split into two groups of five planes each, and attacked the bombers. The Germans turned around to escape trouble, but did not get away fast enough and a fierce dogfight ensued. Ed Toppins, Freddie Hutchins, Leonard Jackson shot down a plane. William Green had a confirmed and unconfirmed kill. Weldon Groves shared a kill with a Mustang from another group. Luther Smith and Roger Romine had unconfirmed kills. Charles Jackson, of the 100th Fighter Squadron, was shot down, but he evaded the Germans and returned to the group on 28 August.

On 27 July, the 47th BW was escorted on a mission to an arms factory near Budapest. The fighters were attacked by twenty-five Me-109s and

Private First Class, John T. Fields, an armorer, inspects the ammunition in the P-51 Mustang he services. (Courtesy of National Archives and Records Administration)

FW-190s north of Lake Balaton. The Me-109s initiated the attack, followed by the FW-190s. Lieutenant Emmory Robbins, of the 302nd Fighter Squadron, was shot down. Edward Gleed and Alfred Gorham shot down two planes. Richard Hall, Leonard Jackson, Claude Govan and Felix Kirkpatrick shot down one airplane.

On 28 July, the 55th BW was escorted to Ploesti. On the 30th, forty-three P-51s escorted the 5th BW to the Tokol arms factory near Budapest. An ANR Reggiane re.2001 was seen, flying parallel to the P-51 flown by Carl Johnson. He was warned and the Re.2001 made a turn and tried a 90-degree deflection shot. Johnson shot down the Reggiane. This was before linking up with the bombers. An Me-109 was spotted, but could not be engaged, because it was shot down by a P-51 from another group.

On 31 July, the 47th BW bombed Ploesti and 65 Mustangs took to the air. The mission went well, after the bombers and fighters managed to link up.

On 2 August, the mission was to accompany the 5th BW to Le Pousin oil storage facility and the Portes Les Valences railway marshalling yard

Edward C. Gleed, the Group Operations Officer. (Courtesy of Library of Congress)

in South France. 50 Me-109s had been reported to gather in the area of Toulon. However, when the fighters approached, no hostile aircraft was seen. Despite the lack of action, the mission was not without wounded, as Earl Sherard suffered burns when he crashed his P-51.

On 3 August, the 5th BW attacked the Ober Raderach chemical works. Four Me-109s were spotted, but they did not engage the bombers.

On the 6th, the group had two missions to complete. The main mission was the escorting of bombers of the 55th BW, going to Avignon. One B-24 was shot down by antiaircraft artillery. A group of eight Mustangs was escorting a B-25 back to Italy, after it had landed in Yugoslavia.

On 7 August, sixty-nine P-51s took off, and fifty-four of them carried out the mission. The goal was to bomb the oil refineries at Blechhammer.

A lone Me-109 made a pass at the bombers and then fled the scene. Alfred Gorham, of the 301st Fighter Squadron, got lost on return trip. He eventually landed as Lesina Airfield, where the 325th Fighter Group was stationed. He undershot the runway, which was not equipped with airfield lights, and crashed into Lake Lesina. His plane caught fire, but Gorham survived.

On 9 August, five P-51s escorted the 5th BW as it attacked the Gyer aircraft and car works in Hungary. When going back, Alfonso Simmons, of the 100th Fighter Squadron, jumped out of his plane. His aircraft had been damaged by flak. He joined up with partisans and returned to the group.

On 10 August, the 332nd Fighter Group escorted the 304th BW as they attacked oil refinery in Ploesti.

On 12 August, the 332nd Fighter Group received orders to knock out radar stations around the harbor in Marseilles in anticipation of operation Dragoon. The squadrons were assigned their own targets. These were properly defended.

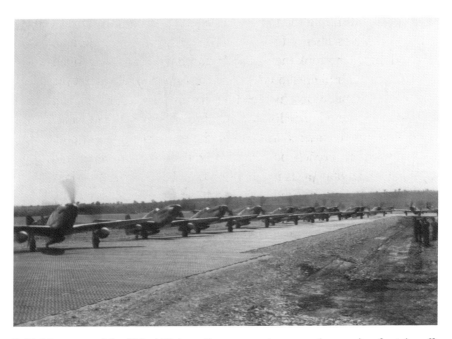

P-51 Mustangs of the 332nd Fighter Group warming up and preparing for take off. Each aircraft is equipped with extra fuel tanks to provide additional range to escort the bombers to their destination. (Courtesy of National Archives and Records Administration)

The 99th Fighter Squadron attacked and destroyed both stations in Montpelier and Sete. While strafing, the P-51 of Dick Macon was damaged and he was forced to jump out of his plane. At low altitude he jumped out and the P-51 crashed into a house. Macon recounted in a newspaper:

> Maybe it was fortunate that I was unconscious when the miracles happened or else, I might have done something wrong and been killed. I was skimming along at 300ft when I ran head-on into a cloud of flak. The burst sliced my aileron controls and flipped my plane over as quickly as you flip a magazine page. While fighting to right the Mustang I suddenly felt a terrific blast of heat, my entire engine smothered out in flames. I passed out.
>
> In the cockpit, the pilot slumped forward, against the control stick. The burning plane went into an outside loop and tossed pilot out of his plane, 300ft above the ground. In the little height from the ground, Macon's parachute opened, limiting the impact of his fall. [...] When I came to 45 minutes later, I found myself looking at three German soldiers who took me to a field hospital where I was found to have a broken shoulder and a broken neck. They set the shoulder but didn't have time to fix my back due to the fact that we were hurriedly evacuated to escape the Americans. Two weeks later I arrived in Sagan, Germany, hospital staffed by French personnel. My neck was X-rayed and set, and again I was moved, this time because the Russians were closing in. Finally, I was liberated at Meuseburg by the 7th Army.[37]

Macon fully recovered.

The 100th engaged their targets as expected. The 301st attacked targets around Toulon. Lieutenant Langdon E. Johnson of the 100th Fighter Squadron crashed into the sea after being hit by flak. Joseph Gordon was shot down and killed.

The 302nd strafed radar installations at Leucate and Narbonne. While they attacked their target, the flight of Alton Ballard, John Daniels, Virgil Richardson and Alexander Jefferson encountered heavy flak.

Daniels splashed into the harbor, which was not advised, as the air scoop could pull the plane under the surface and the pilot would drown before he could climb out of his cockpit. As Alexander Jefferson recounted about his experiences:

> By this time, we were down to 300ft, flying at more than 400 mph. Looking ahead, I could see the first flight of four getting hits on the towers and veering out to sea. Right behind them came the second and third flights, which also got their hits and banked out to sea. Then we came into position. With the target in range, my ship was bucking and shaking. Anti-aircraft fire was coming up on all sides. My oil pressure and coolant temp needles were in the red, with everything else at the top of the green, about to go red.
>
> As I passed over the target at about 50ft, I felt a loud thump shake the plane. I glanced at the instrument panel, and now everything was in the red. I felt a tremendous rush of air. I looked up, and there was a hole in the top of my canopy just in front of my head. I thought: "What the hell?!" Fire and smoke were filling the cockpit. I looked down and saw that flames were coming up through a hole in the floor between my feet and scorching my gloves and boots. I pulled up into a loop to get some altitude, jerked the red knob on the instrument panel, and popped the canopy. At the same time, I racked in the forward trim tab on the elevator with my left hand. At the top of the loop, I punched the safety belt release and let go of the stick. The forward trim tab was supposed to pitch the nose down, but because the plane was upside down, the nose went up abruptly, and I was thrown out. I figure I got out at about 800ft.
>
> I can still see the tail, including the rivets, as it went whizzing by. During the nine months of training, due to the war, we never had a minute on how to bail out of a plane. I looked down and saw the trees. I pulled the D-ring. I looked at it in my hand and thought, "Some SOB sold the silk." The rumor back at base was that someone had been stealing the silk out of the parachutes and selling it to the Italians.

So, when my chute did not immediately open, I thought that had happened to me. But just then my chute popped, and all I could see was green. I fell through some trees and hit squarely on my feet and rolled over. I sustained cuts and bruises on my arms and legs. Fortunately, I was wearing paratrooper boots, which gave extra support to my ankles.[38]

Together with Daniels and Macon, Jefferson ended up in captivity.

On 13 August, the railway bridges near Avignon were attacked by the 304th BW. The group put sixty-one P-51s in the air to escort the bombers to their targets and back. Later that day, new strafing missions were assigned. The 99th and 100th flew fighter sweeps near the Toulon area. A flight of the 100th Fighter Squadron got lost and tried to regain their bearings. They were attacked by two Me-109s and two FW-190s and engaged in combat. However, the attackers and attacked changed roles. While getting out of the ambush, George Rhodes shot down an Me-109.

The 301st and 302nd Fighter Squadron attacked radar installations near Cap Blanc, Camerat Capet, and La Ciotat. The antenna came toppling down and the six buildings nearby were strafed. Two airplanes were lost. Robert O'Neil, of the 100th Fighter Squadron, went down in a spin. He was reported as missing, but was actually rescued by the Free French. He returned to the unit later. Clarence Allen jumped out of his damaged plane over Elba. He, too, was rescued.

On 15 August, Operation Dragoon finally started. That day the 332nd Fighter Group was escorting bombers of the 55th BW on a mission to southern France. Two enemy Me-109s were seen, but they did not engage. Wilson Eagleson had been hit in the engine by flak. He was losing coolant, but tried to push his plane homewards as long as possible. When he was over Allied territory a squad of American soldiers saw him bail out. When Eagleson had landed and walked to a nearby road, they were waiting with a jeep to bring him back to Ramitelli.

On the 16th, the bombers of the 55th BW were escorted when they attacked the Ober Raderach chemical works in Germany. Herbert Clark, of the 99th Fighter Squadron, was forced to jump out of his plane after it had been damaged by flak. He avoided captivity and finally ended up commanding a band of partisans that harassed the Germans in northern Italy. Clark reunited with the 332nd Fighter Group on 7 May 1945.

On 17 August, Mustangs of the 332nd Fighter Group guided the 304th BW to Ploesti. The next day they escorted the 5th BW to Ploesti. On 19 August another mission went to Ploesti. P-51s guided the bombers of the 47th BW. Twenty minutes after take-off, William Thomas crashed on Pianosa, an Italian island, and got away safely.

Staff Sergeant William Accoo washes down a P-51 Mustang. (Courtesy of National Archives and Records Administration)

On 20 August, fifty-nine P-51s escorted the 5th BW to Oswiecim in Poland. The group was harassed by eighteen Me-109s and FW-190s, but no bombers were attacked.

On 21 August, fifty-two P-51s escorted the 55th BW to the Kornenburg oil refinery, near Vienna. The bombers were late for the rendezvous and the group circled in the air until they arrived. Twenty Me-109s were spotted near Lake Balaton. A single Spitfire was spotted over the target area, it pointed its nose at the bombers and a flight of P-51s made a firing pass at the Spitfire, which rapidly waggled its wings and sped away. That same day six C-47s were escorted to Yugoslavia, and returned with prisoners of war from Yugoslavia to Italy.

On 23 August, the 55th BW needed an escort for their attack on Markersdorf airfield in Germany. The bombers were attacked by fourteen Me-109s. William Hill shot one of them however, the mission was not without incident, when "One B-24 [was] sighted going down in flames in target area."[39]

On 24 August, the P-51s of the 332nd Fighter Group took to the air to escort the 5th BW to Pardubice airfield in Czechoslovakia. Lieutenant Charles McGee had spotted an FW-190 and engaged it. The pilot saw the P-51 coming for him and dived. A series of evasive maneuvers were attempted to shake off his pursuer, but in vain. McGee fired and hit the fighter, which crashed into the ground. McGee was fired upon by anti-aircraft guns from the airfield. He sped away, fired at a locomotive that stood at a rail stop, and climbed to rejoin his group.

Lieutenant William Thomas saw an FW-190 which tried to escape a fight, but Thomas did not let him get away. He chased his prey and fired at it several times, until it eventually went down and crashed into the earth.

During the return trip an Me-109 attacked John Briggs' flight from behind. The P-51s turned to engage their attacker. The fighter was fired upon by Briggs. He saw no result and from behind and below he fired upon the fighter. At the distance of 25 yards, he opened fire again. Pieces of the Me-109 flew back and the pilot bailed out shortly.

On 25 August, the 332nd Fighter Group escorted B-17s of the 5th BW to Brno airfield. The attack went as planned and no hostile fighters took off to engage the bombers.

On 26 August, fifty-six P-51s went with the 304th BW for an attack at Banasea in Bulgaria. Instead of striking their target, nearby woods were bombed. Henry Wise jumped out of his smoking plane after the oil pressure dropped. He was taken prisoner and this caused an unusual situation. Bulgaria switched sides shortly after the Soviet Union crossed the border on 8 September and Wise was left behind. Through Turkey and Egypt, he eventually arrived in Italy, where he joined up with the 332nd Fighter Group. He received promotion and was sent on home. On the same day, Robert O'Neil also returned to the unit after having evaded the Germans in France.

On 27 August, fifty-seven Mustangs took off to escort the 304th and 55th BW to Blechhammer, Germany. A lone German aircraft was seen taking off from an airfield near Prostejov, Czechoslovakia. The American fighters went down and attacked this airfield, just as the one near Kosteletz. Since there was no flak available, the American pilots could strafe many German planes. In the end, when their ammunition had run out, thirteen JU-52s, four JU-87s and three HE-111s were destroyed, and nine JU-52s, four JU-87s, four HE-111s and an Me-323 Gigant damaged, strafing a locomotive that was near the airfield.

On 28 August, the 332nd Fighter Group escorted the 47th BW in a raid to Miskolc, a railway marshalling yard, Yugoslavia. James Walker, who had been missing, returned safely to the unit.

On 29 August, the P-51s took to the skies and went along with the 5th BW attack on Bohumin and Prisover oil refineries and the Morvaska railway marshalling yard. Emile Clifton had to bail out because of engine trouble; he returned to the fighter group at the beginning of September.

On 30 August, the 332nd Fighter Squadron was going to Grosswardein, in Romania. The fighters located an airfield in Grosswardein where the German aircraft were camouflaged poorly underneath stacks of hay. Although there was anti-aircraft artillery present, the squadrons attacked. The result was eighty-three aircraft destroyed and thirty-one damaged. Thirty JU-88s, twelve HE-111s, seven FW-189s, six JU-87s, six DO-217s, five JU-52s, four FW-190s, three Me-109s, three Gotha Go 242 gliders, two Me-323s, two Me-210s, two Me-110s and an Ar 96. It was the most destructive day in the history of the 332nd Fighter Group. Charles Williams, of the 301st, was reported missing. He had been taken prisoner and spent the rest of the war as a POW.

On 31 August, the 332nd split into two formations. One was to escort the 5th BW bombers in two separate waves: the 100th and the 301st Fighter

Squadron escorted the second wave of bombers to Popesti airfield, while the 99th and 302nd escorted the third wave of bombers. These bombers had been modified to carry back prisoners of war. After Romania had switched sides on 23 August 1944, it continued to fight alongside the Soviet Union and the US prisoners of war were gathered at an airfield.

Lieutenant Colonel James Gunn of the 454th Bomb Group had been downed over Ploesti on 17 August and after Romania switched sides on 23 August, he made contact with the Romanian Captain Constatin Cantacuzino. Together the two flew to Foggia in an Me-109, with Gunn in the fuselage, with a painted American flag on the plane. A bold plan was made and between 31 August and 3 September, 1,166 POWs were lifted out of Romania by the 5th BW. Providing escorts for the bombers during this airlift were fighters of the 332nd Fighter Group.

On 1 September, the bombers were escorted to Pitesti, Romania, but due to a combination of inclement weather and navigational errors, the 301st and 302nd did not complete this mission. On 2 September, the 332nd Fighter Group performed an armed reconnaissance in Serbia.

On 3 September, the 332nd Fighter Group escorted the 304th BW and its B-24s as it attacked the bridges at Szolnol and Szeged. On 4 September the 332nd Fighter Group provided escorts for the 304th BW to Tagliamento Casarsa and Latisana, Italy. On 5 September the 5th BW was escorted, destroying bridges. On 6 September, the 332nd Fighter Group escorted the 5th BW when it attacked a railways marshalling yard in Romania.

On 8 September, the 332nd Fighter Group went to the airfield in Ilandza in Yugoslavia, held by the Luftwaffe. Twenty-three P-51s dropped to the deck to strafe the planes, while fourteen others covered them. Eighteen hostile aircraft were destroyed on the ground: five JU-52s, four JU-88s, three FW-200s, three D-217s, and an Me-109, HE-111, and FW-190. James Calhoun was shot down and killed in the crash.

After this, the P-51s flew to Alibunar, where they strafed parked aircraft. There, fifteen FW-190s, two Me-109s and a SM84 transport were destroyed. On the way back a locomotive was destroyed.

On 10 September a special ceremony took place. The 332nd was assembled at the Ramitelli airfield. General Benjamin O. Davis senior came to hand out the Distinguished Flying Cross to his son, Colonel

Benjamin O. Davis, as well as Captain Joseph Elsberry, First Lieutenant Jack Holsclaw and Clarence Lester. The group was given forty-eight hours off.

On 12 September, the 332nd Fighter Group took to the air to escort the 5th BW, and on 13 September they escorted the 304th BW to Blechhammer North oil refinery. Three German fighters were spotted in the distance, but did not come close. During the mission, Wilbur Long went missing and was taken prisoner by the Germans.

On 17 September, the 332nd Fighter Group went with the 5th BW to the Rakos railways marshaling yards. While on their run, a single twin-engine aircraft was spotted over the city. This plane was identified as an RAF Mosquito.

On the 18th, the 332nd Fighter Group took to the air. The 304th BW went to Budapest to strike the Shell oil refinery and railroad bridges. Again, a Mosquito was seen over the target.

General Benjamin O. Davis Sr. pins the Distinguished Flying Cross on his son, Colonel Benjamin O. Davis, Jr. (Courtesy of National Archives and Records Administration)

On 20 September, the 332nd Fighter Group escorted the bombers of the 304th BW on a mission to Malacky airfield, Czechoslovakia.

On 21 September, the 332nd Fighter Group went on an escort to the Debreczen railway marshalling yards in Hungary. The 5th BW would attack the marshalling yards, but the rendezvous failed. The bombers were ten minutes ahead of schedule and the fighters were delayed by eighteen minutes. They never linked up. The last two groups of bombers were dropping their payload on the target when the P-51s arrived. The Luftwaffe was not seen.

On 22 September, during an escort mission, Leonard Willette lost oil pressure and bailed out. He was later declared killed in action. Chris Newman's P-51 was hit by flak and he managed to fly the plane back as far as the Adriatic Ocean, before his engine caught fire and he bailed out. Newman was rescued and returned to the fighter group.

On 23 September, the 332nd Fighter Group went with the 5th BW to attack a synthetic oil factory in Brux, Germany.

On 24 September, the P-51s escorted the 304th to the airfield near Athens. The planes were fired upon by flak and the four warships that resided there. The missions became routine and little air opposition was seen.

On 4 October, four P-51s escorted three C-47s to Sofia, where they circled in the air, while the planes landed and then brought them back to safety. Other C-47s were escorted to Bucharest and back.

Later that day the 332nd Fighter Group took off, to strafe the Greek airfields at Tatoi, Kalamaki and Eleusis. The pilots of the 99th, 100th, and 301st split up to attack the three airfields. The pilots of the 99th went to Tatoi, of the 100th to Kalamaki airfield, and of the 301st to Eleusis airfield.

At Tatoi the 99th found twenty-five to thirty hostile airplanes parked and dispersed from each other. The pilots dropped down and strafed from below. Erwin Lawrence, the squadron commander, hit a cable that had been put over the airfield as a simple form of air defense; his plane turned over and crashed. Lieutenant Kenneth Williams also crashed and was taken prisoner. Herman Lawson claimed a Ju-52 destroyed. Nearly all the other planes were damaged.

The 100th attacked Kalamaki, destroying three planes and damaging eight more. The 301st destroyed four Ju-52s and an SM.79.

Two days later, on 6 October, the Greek airfields at Tatoi, Kalamaki and Eleusis, as well as the airfield Megara were struck once again. The group was led by Colonel Davis. After taking off, the P-51 of Elbert Hudson made a belly-landing at Biferano. It was a bad start to the mission.

The airfield at Tatoi was attacked by the 99th. They destroyed two Ju-52s, a He-111, and an FW-200. Two other planes were damaged, but the attack came not without a cost. The plane of Carl Woods was set on fire by flak and he bailed out, spending the remainder of the war in captivity.

At Eleusis, the Germans had evacuated all their aircraft. Just a Ju-52 remained. The pilots of the 301st attacked the base and a fuel dump was set on fire. Joe Lewis went down trailing smoke and was captured. Andrew Marshall's plane was hit by flak and he bailed out. He had more luck than Woods and Lewis, because Marshall evaded captivity and returned to the group on 18 October.

Lieutenant Andrew D. Marshall had his plane shot up by flak during a strafing mission, but managed to return to the 332nd Fighter Group. (Courtesy of National Archives and Records Administration)

A close-up of Lieutenant Andrew D. Marshall after his return to the 332nd Fighter Group. (Courtesy of National Archives and Records Administration)

At Megara, the airfield was empty, but still engaged by the fighters. The pilots flew in and Freddie Hutchins engaged an ammunition dump, which exploded ferociously. His P-51 was riddled by flak and small arms fire. As he pressed himself down against the armored plate, a burst came through the cockpit and fragments struck his legs.

Hutchins crashed down with his plane not far from Megara and was knocked out. When he woke, he was still strapped in, although his engine, wings, and tail were gone. His flight goggles had been smashed into his forehead and his legs were wounded by fragments. With the aid of Greek civilians, Hutchins was brought to a doctor and from there eventually returned to the group on 23 October.

On 7 October, the 332nd Fighter Group took to the skies and escorted the 5th BW to Lobau oil refinery in Austria. This mission did not go as expected. On their way to the target, Robert Wiggins made a crash-landing with his plane and Carl Woods went missing in an overcast sky, never to be heard from again. Roosevelt Stiger had problems with his oxygen and later crashed down in the Adriatic Sea. He was not seen to escape

Benjamin O. Davis and another officer of the 332nd Fighter Group playing chess in the officers' club at Ramitelli air base. (Courtesy of Library of Congress)

and his body was never recovered. Eventually, twenty-three pilots had been forced to land at forward airfields, and needed picking up.

On 11 October, after three days of rest, the group went to Budapest and from there to Bratislava along the Danube, harassing rivercraft and railroad traffic. Just twenty out of the seventy-two planes could complete their missions. The rest were unable to locate their targets. When they found gaps in the clouds near Esztergom, Hungary, they destroyed seventeen hostile aircraft at three different airfields. The pilots also destroyed an oil wagon, a fuel dump, and two locomotives. Six barges, another train, and a goods wagon were damaged. Lieutenant George Rhodes had a forced landing and his P-51 was not worth salvaging, but at least he was safe.

On 12 October, the 332nd Fighter Group took off and again searched the same area. While flying over hostile territory, a report came in that a biplane was seen flying over the Kaposvas airfield and fourteen planes of the 99th Fighter Squadron were sent over to investigate. Between thirty-five to forty aircraft were located, parked around the airfield. The 99th attacked and eighteen planes were left burning on the ground. This included five He-111s, five Ju-88s, four Me-109s, an FW-190, an FW-200, another unidentified twin-engine airplane and a trainer. Five more planes were damaged.

The 302nd Fighter Squadron received a similar report, that a He-111 had been seen near another airfield. The group located hostile aircraft climbing at two o'clock below them. They went into the attack, but were jumped by nine Me-109s covering two He-111s.

Within fifteen minutes the three German He-111s and six of the nine Me-109s were destroyed. During the fight, the planes had descended all the way to the ground and the pilots explained that the Germans used poor, or in some cases none at all, evasive tactics. Afterwards, the airfield was attacked and eight airplanes were destroyed on the ground, as well as four more damaged.

On their way to their intended targets, the 100th and the 301st encountered yellow-tailed P-51s. These turned into them, as if to attack, but thankfully a friendly fire incident was prevented.

The 100th Fighter Squadron attacked a railway and a factory, where three trains were damaged. The 301st attacked oil barges on the Danube. Three sank, while eleven were damaged. Walter McCreary was hit by flak and he jumped out of his plane. For the rest of the war, he was a POW.

On 13 October, the 332nd Fighter Group escorted the 304th BW to Blechhammer South oil refineries. After this mission had been completed, the group proceeded to drop down to the deck and scour for targets of opportunity. A train heading east from Bratislava was attacked and two trains as well as a flat car were damaged. Another train was strafed, in which the locomotive was destroyed and goods and coal cars damaged. A small house beside the track being used for storing ammunition exploded after being strafed.

At the Tapolcza airfield seven more airplanes were destroyed, consisting of three HE-111s, three JU-52s, and an FW-189.

Walter Westmoreland, of the 302nd Fighter Squadron, was killed in a plane crash and William Green jumped out of his plane after it suffered damage in an explosion. He managed to evade captivity and returned to the group. Less lucky was his wingman Luther Smith.

A flight of four pilots, including Smith and Green, were flying back after their attack on an enemy airfield. At this location, Smith had destroyed two enemy bombers on the ground. During their flight, they spotted a freight yard. The two other pilots first strafed the yard, while Smith and Green provided cover. Smith was eager to return home, but Green dove down to attack and Smith followed him in the attack.

In an interview years later, Smith recounted:

> Nevertheless, I followed him down, but I felt there wasn't any real opportunities left because these other two fellows had pretty much hit the freight yard and hit all the vehicles that had oil in them or whatever there was in the vehicles to get them to burn. Not all the cars were burning. So, when I followed my wingman down, I was right behind him, he made his pass. I started to shoot at the cars too and my reaction was getting some strikes on these vehicles just to add a little compliment to the two bombers you've actually got on your gun camera. So, when I was only about 10ft over the tops of the cars. Pretty low. So, I lined up on it and noticed the tracer bullets were going directly into the cars. Oh, I've got a pretty good strike on these. So, I just held the trigger and said, "Let me hold this for just a second or more and then rise up and we'll join up and we'll head for home." Got

halfway down the line of cars and there's a huge, monstrous explosion. So big I couldn't fly over it. As I said, I was only about 10ft over the tops of the cars. Flying about 300 miles an hour. And I couldn't fly to either side. The explosion was much larger than I could escape. So, I thought, "You've done it this time! You're not going to make this." Fearing that, as I flew through the explosion, steel and debris and everything else was going to be rising up and hit the airplane and cause fatal destruction of both me and the airplane. But fortunately, because God was with me, I was in and out of the explosion just very quick. Then I was afraid it was going to take out my engine and destroy the airplane in some way. And the concussion from the explosion did blow out the glass of my cockpit, except for the windshield. It was pretty sturdy. It was bulletproof. It also buckled the wings and tore off part of the tail. Just from the concussion from the explosion. It was pretty violent. Because I was only—I don't know how far I was from the explosion, but it was just in front of me. Must have been about 100ft, I guess, and I flew right through it. But the aircraft engine was operating. The instruments were functioning when I got through the explosion and I could see, you made it. But the glass, remaining glass, in the cockpit and the windshield, the front glass, was blackened by the explosion and the smoke. So, I couldn't really see out.[40]

Despite leaking oil and the damage, Smith climbed back up in the air, under the assumption that he might still make it home. As he continues his story:

The airplane was just rocked by the concussion. I was checking the instruments to make sure the airplane— Because the airplane was partially turned on its back. I had failed to remember that part of the tail assembly had been blown off in the explosion and the airplane was flying so slow because the engine was frozen and the propeller was barely windmilling. The airplane was flying pretty slow.

The airplane fell into a tailspin. Couldn't stay in flying speed and fell into a tailspin. Now the airplane is on fire in a tailspin. And I'm caught in the airplane with my seatbelt fastened, because I hadn't released it. Wasn't going to do that until I got it on its back. I think I had just unbuckled my safety belt as I turned the airplane on its back because what happened to me was, I slid partially out of the airplane as it fell into the tailspin. I knew I couldn't get out of this airplane in a tailspin, so I tried to get back into the cockpit with my seatbelt partially holding me in and there wasn't anything I could hang onto with the canopy jettisoned. I was partially upside down in the tailspin. I was really in a dilemma and a mess, too. I was trying to scramble and the only thing I could do was to reach with my right foot and hook my foot between the rudder bar and the brake of the airplane. I was able to wedge my foot between the rudder bar and the brake. It's just a lever. And that caught my foot, my right foot. But it kept me in the airplane. It also jammed me so the airplane was spinning up—the spin speed was beginning to speed up and the torque was increasing. I couldn't get out of the airplane and couldn't free my foot and get out of the airplane or get back in it. It was pulling me out of the airplane. I was in a real dilemma.[41]

I was coming down. Straight down. In a tailspin. So, the final thought I can remember before I went unconscious was, "So this is how guys go." And I can remember that as though it was this morning. […] After being able to get out of the explosion, after being able to escape from the ground fire in the strafing mission, this was the third event and I said, "This one you're not going to make." And so, what happened was, because I was partially out of the cockpit of the airplane, my oxygen mask was blown off by the wind because I was halfway out of the cockpit. I went unconscious.[42]

I was in the parachute coming down. Head first. Normally in the parachute you're sitting upright. I'm coming down head first. So, the thing that I see because I'm coming down head first is looking straight up at the canopy of my parachute, which is ripped. Right through the front of the canopy. So, when I came to, I was in a total state of shock. Had no understanding of where I was. I wasn't aware of the parachute. I was in an airplane. Then the silence. No engine noise was what struck me first. It was just the swishing of air. Me being in the parachute. […] I'd never been in a parachute before in my life. Something horrible had happened and I was in a state of shock so I couldn't feel anything. I was trying to make an assessment of what could have happened. I happened to glance down to the ground and directly underneath me was my airplane. Maybe 10,000ft below. But I could see my airplane burning on the ground. So, I knew that I had escaped out of the airplane. Didn't know how. But I was out of the airplane in a parachute coming down head first rather than sitting upright in the parachute harness. Then I said, "How did you get here?" So, I was trying to make a quick assessment. Something must have happened to me. If you look at the parachute, the canopy being ripped. What obviously happened was that the—after sixty years I've obviously thought this thing through—so while I was in the airplane, the airplane was in a tailspin. I was halfway out of the airplane and I was unconscious. I still pull the ripcord, which you obviously don't do in an airplane. Because it was a seat pack that I'm sitting on. There is what they call a pilot chute, which is not much larger than a handkerchief and a spring. So, when you pull the pack and you pull the ripcord of the pack, it releases this—there's a spring on it. It opens it up like unfolding a handkerchief. That's what pulls out the main canopy. And because I was partially out of the airplane and I pulled the ripcord of the parachute, the pilot chute was able to come out and pull the main canopy out of the cockpit, and because the airplane was in a tailspin and not coming straight down the uneven gyration enabled the canopy of the parachute to get out without entangling totally on the airplane fuselage, but it did entangle somewhat because it ripped the center of the parachute canopy.[43]

I was coming down head first. Like a bag of coal. So, then I said, "You're not going to make it after all." All this is happening [at] lightning speed. I went unconscious a second time. While I was unconscious, I was in a dream, a very agitated nightmarish kind of a dream that I was in a room, confined in a room. Couldn't control myself and I was banging my head against the wall because of the agitated situation I was in. I was just banging my head against the wall. Uncontrollably. In reality what was happening was I was crashing down through the trees. The canopy of my parachute was coming to rest on the top of the trees, […] I came to and I came to realize I was crashing down through the trees and the canopy was slowing my speed down. Reached out and grabbed a branch and sat on it. I was alive. That was the fourth incident that saved my life. Landing in a tree rather than on the ground, and break my back or my neck.[44]

I could see [my wingman], because he was flying right over the top of the trees. The bullets were going off from my airplane. He was attracting attention from German soldiers on the ground. They were shooting at him and shooting at me. All of a sudden, I didn't see him anymore. The bullets were still going off and I could see bullets whipping through the trees, hitting leaves and that sort of thing. So, they were still shooting at me and I was trying to figure out why are they shooting at me. I can't even get out of this tree. They thought I was hiding. So eventually the Germans saw my body, my person in the tree. They figured there must be something wrong. So, one of the German soldiers climbed the tree. Speaking German. He was speaking to me. I didn't know what he was saying. He was calling to his buddies. This guy is injured. Couldn't get out of the tree, and he needed help. […] The tree was about 100ft tall and I was up about 70ft, where I was sitting on a branch. Another German soldier came up the tree and he had a rope. So, he put the rope underneath my armpits and lowered me down this tree. I couldn't control my leg, my right hip which was in two pieces; every time it struck a branch, I couldn't control it.

[…] It was a compound fracture, and the two hip bones, two pieces of hip bone had protruded through the skin and were outside of my leg when I was finally on the ground. Obviously, the pain was beyond description. I thought I was going to be able to faint again and get out of that pain experience, but I couldn't. I was still conscious.[45]

Smith went through a series of German hospitals, suffered bone infections and dysentery. He was eventually liberated at the end of the war.

On 14 October the 332nd Fighter Group took off and escorted the 49th BW to Odertal oil refineries. There was no opposition. Rual Bell, of the 100th Fighter Squadron, suffered mechanical issues, his oil temperature was high and his fuel was low. Attempts to restart the engine were in vain and jumped out of his plane. He spent the first night in the woods and met a Yugoslavian farmer the next day, who informed the partisans. He was picked up by a British warship and returned to the squadron in December 1944.

On 16 October, the 5th BW was escorted to the Brux oil refiners and one Mustang was damaged by flak. Colonel Davis led the mission.

On 17 October, three Mustangs went along with a lone B-17 of the 5th BW to escort it to Bucharest. Later, fifty-two P-51s of 332nd Fighter Group took off to escort the 5th BW to Blechhammer oil refinery, but one of them returned early with mechanical problems. They saw only a single Mosquito south of Brno.

On 20 October, sixty-four airplanes took off to escort the 5th BW to Brux oil refineries and fifty-one completed the mission. The Luftwaffe was not seen; however, they did see friendly B-26 bombers near Venice. A Catalina flying boat went out later that day, escorted by two P-51s to locate seven survivors from a B-17 that had been ditched. One of the planes had to return due to a lack of fuel, but the other guided the boat back to shore.

On 21 October, the 304th BW was escorted by fifty-four P-51s of the 332nd Fighter Group planes. Four more had taken off, but returned due to mechanical issues. The mission was Gyor, Hungary. Captain Vernon Haywood went out later with three other P-51s out to locate downed fliers. They saw two men in floating vests and they stayed in the area until the two persons were picked up by an RAF Walrus.

On 23 October, the 304th BW was escorted to Regensburg. Shelby Westbrook had mechanical issues and returned to the airfield with

Lieutenant Chandler as his escort. However, they crash landed their planes before reaching friendly lines. They evaded captivity and eventually returned to the group.

On 29 October, Alfonza Davis, commander of the 99th Fighter Squadron, was killed while escorting a converted version of the P-38, on a reconnaissance mission in the area of Munich. Davis probably suffered from oxygen deprivation. William Campbell became the new CO. It was one of the four missions that day. Bombers of the 49th BW were escorted and during the return flight, Fred Brewers plane stalled and he went missing.

In October, the 332nd lost fifteen pilots. With so many pilots lost and not enough replacements arriving, the fact that Black pilots had to fly more missions than white pilots remained unchanged.

On 1 November, the 304th BW was escorted to Vienna and two supply drops went to partisans in Yugoslavia. One of the flights lost the C-47 it was escorting after turning to identify approaching airplanes, that turned out to be P-38s. Once identification was made, the C-47 had disappeared into the clouds and it was not seen at the target area either.

A Tuskegee Airmen with two Italian ladies near Ramitelli Airfield. (Courtesy of Craig Huntly)

On 3 November, Colonel Davis returned to the USA and Major George Roberts took over. Weather problems prevented many operations. On 4 November the 332nd Fighter Group took off, escorting the 5th BW in their attack on Regensburg oil storage facility.

During this mission a P-51, with the same group markings as the 332nd Fighter Group came up, but lacking the side numbers. The plane joined the formation for forty-five minutes, before it turned northeast towards Trieste and disappeared. Two lone P-38s were escorted. One to Linz and the other to Munich.

On 5 November, forty-eight P-51s went with the 5th BW to Floridsdorf oil refinery in Austria. That evening there were two more P-38s to be escorted. During one of these missions, the formation was engaged by flak. The planes scattered and no radio contact could be established with the P-38.

On 6 November, the 5th BW was escorted to Moosbierbaum oil refinery in Vienna. The 332nd Fighter Group participated in this mission. William Faulkner's P-51 was seen falling out of formation and he was initially listed as missing, before being declared dead. It is believed his oxygen tank had failed and he passed out from hypoxia.

On 7 November, William Campbell took charge of the sixty-three P-51s that escorted the 55th BW to Trento and Bolzano. Four of the P-51s suffered flak damage.

On 11 November, the missions resumed. Fifty-two P-51s escorted the 5th BW in their attack on the Brux oil refineries. Flak over Salzburg was dense and Lieutenant Elton Nightingale went missing during the mission. He became separated from his wingmate in the clouds and proceeded to fly back to base, where he never arrived. The P-51 of Turner Payne was also experiencing trouble and he crash landed at Lesina. The P-51 was ruined, but he was safe.

Poor weather prevented further missions until 16 November, when the group escorted the 304th BW to Munich West railway marshalling yard. As the planes were taking off from Ramitelli, a farmer led his sheep across the runway; Roger Romine's plane plowed into the animals and he was then rammed by William Hill. Woodrow Crocket, who had been watching the take off, pulled Hill from his wrecked plane. Hill was badly burned by the incident, and Woodrow Crockett would be awarded the Soldier's Medal for his bravery. Sadly, Roger Romine died in the accident.

Woodrow W. Crockett and Edward C. Gleed in Ramitelli, Italy, March 1945. (Courtesy of Library of Congress)

The mission continued and the B-24s were met at Masseria. Two Me-109s were seen south of Latisano. They put themselves up-sun and dived from behind on a flight of six P-51s. They damaged the plane of George Haley, but were chased off by P-51s from the 52nd Fighter Group.

On the way back, Louis Purnell, Luke Weathers and Melvin Jackson saw a crippled B-24 bomber flying in the area of Udine. While protecting the bomber, the flight was attacked by eight Me-109s. They attacked in a string and then made a Lufbery circle for their defense. The planes flew in a horizontal circle, where each airplane covered the aircraft in front of him. The tactic offered some cover against horizontal attacks, but was vulnerable against attacks from above or below. The tactic was introduced during the First World War and by the end of the conflict, it was already considered outdated, as Luke Weathers would show with deadly determination:

126

Captain Weathers peeled off into the formation of Me-109s closing in to the last two to 100 yards and fired short bursts from zero to twenty degrees deflection. One Me-109 began smoking and he followed it to 1,000ft and saw it crash into the ground. Captain Weathers observed an Me-109 closing in on his tail and he chopped throttle and Me-109 overshot. Captain Weathers fell in on the tail of the Me-109 firing short bursts until it crashed into the side of a mountain.[46]

During the mission an unidentified aircraft was seen. Four P-51s turned towards the aircraft and one even opened fire. However, the plane was identified as a British Spitfire, which promptly escaped.

On 17 November, the 332nd Fighter Group guided the 5th BW in their attack on the Brux refineries. Out of the fifty-two P-51s that took off, eight returned early. The bombers and the fighters were delayed by a headwind. One of the fighters returning early came across a P-38 that requested the P-51 to circle over a crashed bomber, until being relieved. Meanwhile, eight parachutes were seen in the water.

On 18 November, P-51s of the 332nd Fighter Group escorted a bombing strike on enemy airfields near Vicenza and Verona. Lieutenant Alva Temple had a problem with his landing gear and belly-landed at Ramitelli after the mission, while Lieutenant Henry R. Peoples went missing.

On 19 November, the group strafed a railway, road vehicles and river crafts in the areas of Gyor, Hungary, and Vienna and Esztergom, Austria. While the 302nd provided cover, the 99th strafed between Gyor and Veszprem. Fifteen horse-drawn wagons were destroyed and twenty goods locomotives. A hundred horse-drawn wagons were damaged, two locomotives, ten trucks and forty goods wagons.

With the 301st providing cover, the 100th Fighter Squadron strafed the rails and roads, destroying one tank wagon and damaging thirty goods wagons. The rivers between Esztergom and Gyor were also scoured and six barges and a tugboat were damaged. Roger Gaiter was hit by flak and he jumped out, becoming a prisoner of war.

After the 100th Fighter Squadron had used up its ammunition, the 301st took over. A German fighter was fired upon and two 88 mm guns were damaged, as well as six more barges. While returning to base, a flak gun damaged Quitman Walker's plane, forcing him to bail out. He became a prisoner of war.

On 20 November, fifty P-51s took off and covered the attacks of the 5th BW and the 55th BW on Blechhammer South oil refinery. Lieutenant Maceo Harris went missing after experiencing coolant problems and never returned. After the war, his body was buried in an American cemetery in Belgium.

Bad weather limited the activities of the group. On 22 November two B-25s were escorted to Pedrograd, Yugoslavia by eight P-51s and on 26 November a reconnaissance flight to Grodenwoh and Nurnberg was escorted.

On 2 December, the 332nd Fighter Group took off to escort the 49th and 55th BW, again to Blechhammer. The coolant of Cornelius Gould's plane failed, causing white glycol vapor to pour out. Gould bailed out and was captured by the Germans, becoming a prisoner of war. The 302nd lost two pilots that day when Earl Highbaugh and James Ramsey crashed during a collision in the air.

On 3 December, the 49th BW was guided to their target by the 332nd Fighter Group. The target was Udine Pass in northern Italy. The bombers were difficult to cover, since they were too strung out. Lieutenant Marion Rodgers crash landed at Ramitelli, but was safe.

On 9 December, fifty-seven airplanes escorted the 5th BW to Brux. A single jet-powered Me-262 made a pass at the fighters, then disappeared. This was the first encounter with the Me-262 fighter, as Davis recalled:

> In December, a month marked by the first appearance of German jets, we flew twenty-two missions. If Hitler had concentrated on building and manning these jet fighters, he could have effectively stopped our bombing operations. The jets were a frightening development, and their advantage over our prop fighters could have been overwhelming. We saw thirteen Me-262s on 9 December; two of them attacked our formation.[47]

It was the first jet-powered airplane and it had spent several years in development. The group was attacked again over Muhldorf by an Me-262, which flew head-on at the P-51. Two groups of Me-262s were seen later to the east of the formation, but did not engage.

On 11 December, the 332nd Fighter Group took off to escort the 47th BW to the Moosbierbaum oil refinery. During the trip a bomber suddenly exploded. Another escort went to Prague, where reconnaissance was conducted by another airplane.

On 15 December, the 47th BW was escorted to Innsbruck by the 332nd Fighter Group. On 16 December P-51s of the 332nd Fighter Group escorted the B-17 bombers of 5th BW to Brux. Two fighters escorted a straggling bomber home, while later five fighters escorted a bomber to Mrkoplj, Yugoslavia. On 17 December, forty P-51s guided the 304th BW to Olomouc. Forty hostile fighters were seen on the ground, unable to take off.

On 18 December, fifty-one P-51s took off to escort bombers to Blechhammer and six of them returned early. The rendezvous initially failed and the majority of the escort was dispatched to the target. Later it turned out that the bombers were delayed and they were escorted to the target. Six P-51s escorted a P-38 on a reconnaissance mission to Innsbruck.

On 19 December, the oil refinery at Blechhammer South was struck again by the 55th BW, which arrived seventeen minutes late at the rendezvous point. The 332nd Fighter Group escorted them to the target, until they had to break off due to a lack of fuel. Another mission guided a reconnaissance plane to Dresden. On 20 December the rendezvous between the 332nd Fighter Group and the bombers of the 5th BW was delayed and this caused problems for the fighters, which had to break off earlier than intended. Two fighters came down at forward airfields due to a lack of fuel. A reconnaissance flight was escorted to Prague.

On 22 December a P-38 was escorted on a reconnaissance mission to Ingolstadt, Germany, by fighters of the 332nd Fighter Group. On 23 December a P-38 was escorted on a reconnaissance flight to Prague. While returning, the plane of Lawrence Dickson of the 100th Fighter Squadron developed engine trouble and he bailed out. His parachute was seen to open, but in the snow it was difficult to locate the white parachute. Lawrence was declared missing in action. His remains were finally recovered in 2018 and reburied in Arlington National Cemetery, Virginia.

On 24 December, Colonel Benjamin Davis returned from America and took command of the Fighter Group. On 25 December the 332nd Fighter

Group escorted bombers to Brux. Out of the forty-six airplanes that took off, four returned due to mechanical issues. While returning, four Me-109s were chasing a group of seven bombers. The Me-109s broke off the attack after two P-51s headed in their direction.

On 26 December, the 332nd Fighter Group escorted the 5th BW and 55th BW on their return trip from their attacks on Blackhammer and Odertal oil refineries.

On 27 December, the bombers of the 5th BW were escorted by the 332nd Fighter Group to Vienna. During the mission a B-17 was seen to explode. On 28 December, the 304th BW was escorted by the 332nd Fighter Group to Kolin and Pardubice in Czechoslovakia. Of the fifty-six aircraft that took off, only six returned.

29 December, was an unusually grim day for the 332nd Fighter Group. On that day the 304th BW was escorted to their targets at Muhldorf and Landshut, Germany. Sixty aircraft took off and five returned early. Eleven fighters were detached to guide a lone B-24 in its attack on Passau. While at the target, Frederick D. Funderberg and Andrew Marshall disappeared, after probably suffering a midair collision or being hit by flak. On the return flight, Robert Friend's aircraft had a mechanical issue and he jumped from his plane. Lewis Craig jumped out as well. Both men returned to the squadron. Eighteen bombers had landed at Ramitelli due to the bad weather, seventeen of the 485th BG and one of the 455th BG. Due to weather issues, on 30 December there were no missions.

As Colonel Davis recounted:

> Suddenly we had more than 200 white visitors scattered throughout our camp, living, eating, and sleeping as best they could under the severely crowded circumstances. Such a mixing of the races would never have been allowed to occur in the United States. Freddie Hutchins, from Waycross, Georgia, and a white B24 pilot from Atlanta were obliged to share a pup tent, and Freddie gave him a liberal education. The B24 pilots were grounded for several days. They enjoyed their stay and learned that, in matters of humanity, we were not any different from them.[48]

Chapter 5

Death of the Luftwaffe

The year 1945 started with a boost for the squadron morale. Brigadier General Dean C. Strother, commander of the XV Fighter Command, came to the 332nd Fighter Group and awarded seven pilots the Distinguished Flying Cross. The decorated officers were: Major Lee Rayford and Captains Melvin T. Jackson, Andrew D. Turner, Dudley Watson, William A. Campbell, George E. Gray, and Vernon Haywood.

Missions resumed again on 3 January 1945, when three P-51s escorted a reconnaissance plane to Munich and Linz. Unfortunately, the mission was abandoned due to cloud cover. On 5 January, a Mosquito was escorted to Munich, Germany.

On 8 January, the group would strike at the railway marshalling yard in Linz. The bombers of the 47th BW would attack the target. The mission failed as the bombers and fighters were unable to locate each other in the thick clouds.

On 15 January, another mission was attempted. This time the fifty-two P-51s had to link up with the bombers of the 304th BW, but did not find them. They did find bombers of the 47th BW, linked up with them and escorted them as far as possible before returning home.

On 18 January, another series of reconnaissance flights failed. The clouds over Stuttgart were too thick. The same happened over Prague, preventing the two separate flights from making their photo runs. The only one successful run was over Munich.

On 19 January, a P-38 was escorted by the 332nd Fighter Group to Prague. The pilot of the P-38 developed engine trouble and jumped out of his aircraft. On 20 January four P-51s escorted a reconnaissance plane to Prague. While returning, the planes encountered a snow storm. They lost each other and all returned to base. That same day the 332nd Fighter Group escorted the 5th BW to Regensburg.

On 21 January, forty-four P-51s escorted the 5th BW in its attack on Austria. The bombers and pilots finally linked up. Two Me-262s were encountered, but luckily, they remained at a distance. A P-51 was damaged and Samuel J. Foreman and Albert L. Young were reported missing at first, and later as casualties. Young's corpse was discovered in the vicinity of his plane. A theory is that he bailed out, but due to the low altitude, his parachute did not have time to fully open. Foreman had reported engine trouble and disappeared. He was later confirmed dead.

Weather kept the planes grounded for several days.

On 31 January, the 47th and 55th BW attacked the Moosbierbaum oil refinery in Austria. The two bombers' wings arrived late, and the P-51 escorts were divided into two groups to provide adequate coverage.

On 1 February, a special attack was made at Moosbierbaum. 100th and 301st escorted the 49th BW, which could not locate their target. The escorts eventually needed to return, after handing over their charges to another escort group. The 99th and 302nd launched later that day. They guided the 47th BW to Graz.

On 3 February, four P-51s of the 332nd Fighter Group escorted a P-38 on a reconnaissance flight to Munich, Germany. On 5 February the group guided the 47th BW to Salzburg. The Salzburg Main Railway Station was attacked. Due to the weather and route to the target, not all the fighters were capable of providing an adequate escort. During the mission, four P-51s with checkered tails were seen escorting four yellow-tailed B-51s.

On 6 February, an intended fighter sweep was disrupted by the clouds. The intention was to clear the way for the delivery of supplies to partisans in Yugoslavia, but this failed. The pilots could also not contact the transport aircraft.

Another attack at Moosbierbaum was made on 7 February. Thirty-three pilots of the 99th and 302nd took off to escort the 304th BW, and twenty-nine pilots later took off from the 100th and 301st to escort the 47th BW bombers. Two P-51s nursed a damaged bomber back.

On 8 February the same mission was attempted as earlier, to deliver supplies to partisans. The weather was good and there were no Germans forces in the area. A British Lysander landed and took off again. That same day the 55th was escorted by forty-one P-51s to Vienna, mingling with bombers of the 304th BW, and a reconnaissance flight went to Stuttgart,

Colonel Benjamin O. Davis Jr., Commander of the 332nd Fighter Group, discusses with two of his pilots a strafing mission that he has just completed. (Courtesy of National Archives and Records Administration)

Germany. A Walrus, a British amphibious bi-plane, was seen circling two dinghies in the water.

On 11 February, another pilot was lost. Thomas C. Street died when his plane crashed into the sea. On 12 February, six P-51s of the 332nd Fighter Group escorted a P-38 on a reconnaissance flight to Prague.

13 February was a busy day for the 332nd Fighter Group, with three missions conducted that day. A P-38 was escorted to Munich, bombers of the 49th BW were escorted to Vienna, and escort was provided for bombers attacking Zagreb, Maribor and Graz.

14 February was another busy day; thirty P-51s escorted the 5th BW in its attack on oil refineries in Austria. Due to clouds the formation scattered; once out of Austria, three P-51s attacked five small river craft on the Drava River. The 55th BW was escorted by thirty-six P-51s to the same target.

On 15 February, two attacks were made by the 49th BW to the Penzinger marshalling yards in Vienna, which had been split up in two groups. The 99th and the 302nd escorted the first force. The 100th and the 301st escorted the second force. The second group encountered a couple of P-38s, which attacked the P-51s in an exchange of friendly fire. A crippled bomber of the 461st BG was also escorted.

More missions were conducted on 16 February, including escorting two reconnaissance flights. Escort was also provided for a P-38 and, separately, a Mosquito to Munich. The 332nd Fighter Group escorted bombers of the 5th BW to Lechfield airdrome, but from the forty-nine aircraft that took off, only nine completed the mission. The others were recalled due to bad weather and another airplane landed at a friendly field. Two others performed ad-hoc air-sea rescue, after noting a splash in the sea, being ordered to keep circling the area until a boat had arrived. It turned out that the suspected life raft was a belly tank.[1] John Chavis, of the 99th Fighter Squadron, went missing in the overcast sky. A bomber exploded in the air during this mission, probably hit by flak. Two more bombers also exploded in mid-air, before the mission was over.

On 17 February, two more reconnaissance flights were escorted. Six P-51s escorted a reconnaissance flight to Nurnberg, but the mission was aborted once it was discovered that the camera equipment did not work as intended. Another recon flight went with four Mustangs and a Mosquito to Munich. Forty-six Mustangs took off and forty-four P-51s went towards the railway between Linz-Vienna and strafed trains. Two locomotives, two motor transports on flat cars, three tank cars, and a power transformer were destroyed.

On 18 February, three P-51s escorted a reconnaissance flight to Linz. The 332nd Fighter Group provided escorts for the 47th BW on their mission to Wels to attack a railway marshalling yard. The mission was not accomplished, due to the thick overcast.

On 19 February, forty-eight pilots took off and rendezvoused with the bombers of the 49th BW on a mission to Vienna. Due to headwinds, there was a mix up and some fighters instead of bombers of the 47th BW, 55th, and 304th BW were escorted. A lone British Spitfire was seen, and it acted in a hostile manner, trying to get into the tail of the formation. Three P-51s dropped their tanks and engaged him, forcing the fighter to flee.

On 20 February, another reconnaissance mission was conducted. Five P-51s escorted a P-38 to Nurnberg. The P-38 developed mechanical troubles and the flight returned before reaching their target. Forty-three P-51s took off and escorted the 47th BW to Vipitento and the Brenner marshalling yards. The bombers were not at the agreed location. One squadron was sent ahead while the others waited for the bombers, which eventually were encountered, but the escorts had to return to base due to a lack of fuel. The first group that had been sent ahead escorted the 49th BW in attacking their target.

On 21 February, thirty-nine P-51s escorted the 304th BW to Vienna, attacking the railway yard. A bomber had mechanical issues and was escorted by two P-51s back to safety. The rest of the mission progressed without incident.

On 22 February, the 5th BW attacked a marshalling yard in south-west Germany, escorted by the 332nd Fighter Group. Two escort missions accompanied a reconnaissance flight to Prague and to Stuttgart.

On 23 February, the 304th BW attacked the Gmund marshalling yards, but this was complicated due to the weather. The bombers split up to attack two separate targets. The fighters split up as well. In the clouds, the several fighters lost the bombers they were escorting. Instead, they came across unescorted B-17s of the 5th BW and stuck with them.

Lieutenant Clarence A. Oliphant took off late. He hurried to catch up with the other P-51s ahead of him, but did not link up with them. While in the air, Oliphant saw a formation of P-38s. After gaining permission from the controllers, Oliphant flew in formation with the P-38s, one of which had to return.

When reaching their target in south-east Austria, the P-38s started to drop their bombs on the target. Since Oliphant had no bombs of his own, he dropped both of his drop tanks over the target. How much damage this really did can only be guessed at. After this, Oliphant returned with the P-38s and eventually landed back at his base.[2]

On 24 February, a reconnaissance flight was conducted to Munich. A P-38 took photographs.

On 25 February, forty-five P-51s attacked traffic in the Munich-Linz-Ingolstadt Salzburg area. The 99th, 100th and 301st Fighter Squadron strafed alternatively, while the others provided cover. The 100th went first and struck between Rosenheim, Muhldorf and Landshut. This attack destroyed four locomotives and damaged other train carts. An airfield was spotted and attacked, leaving two HE-111s destroyed and another HE-111 and Me-109 damaged. After the 100th, the 99th went down to attack They destroyed four locomotives and damaged additional carriages. George Iles was hit by flak; his coolant system was damaged and he was taken prisoner.

Wendell Hockaday hit a locomotive with his wing during the strafing. He flew his P-51 as far as the Alps, then bailed out and went missing. His body was recovered in 1949 and buried in Hampton, Virginia. Daniel Rich's sustained second degree burns when his plane crash-landed after being damaged. Lastly, the 301st attacked, destroying a power station, damaging another power station and an electric locomotive. Alfred Gorham bailed out when his plane developed mechanical issues. He was taken prisoner.

On 26 February, three planes provided escort for a Mosquito that took photographs of the Munich area. On 27 February, thirty-two P-51s of the 332nd Fighter Group took off and escorted the 49th BW to Augsburg where they attacked the railway marshalling yard. A single Me-163 was seen in the distance, but it did not approach.

Three missions were flown on 28 February. Twice an escort was provided for a P-38 that went to Prague and the 5th BW was escorted to Verona. The next day, 1 March, would be even busier, with four missions flown. Two were reconnaissance escorts to Stuttgart, another P-38 was escorted to Prague and lastly the B-24s of the 55th BW were escorted to Moosbierbaum oil refineries near Vienna. Arriving at their destination, bad weather prevented the bombers from engaging their target. Instead, they attacked the target at Amstetten. While in the air, the P-51s saw twelve Sturmoviks (Soviet planes) in the vicinity of Lake Balaton, highlighting the fact that Germany was closed in on both sides. Another light brown P-38 was seen in the air, it wiggled its wings as if in recognition.[3] The German territory became smaller and so it was more likely opposition would be encountered. German hostility remained firm in the last months of the war.

On 2 March, a recon flight to Prague was escorted. Thirty-six Mustangs took off to bombers of the 304th BW that went to Linz to attack the railway marshalling yard. Two of the escorts returned early, while the rest continued with the mission. On 3 March the 100th and 301st Fighter Squadron took off to search for trains to strafe between Maribor Bruck and Wiener Neustadt in Austria. While flying along the Maribor-Graz line, four planes of the 100th were sent down to fire at parked carriage, damaging a passenger carriage and seven goods wagons.

Other planes of the 100th searched the area and some strafed an airfield they had located in the vicinity. Robert Martin and Alphonso

Simmons were shot down. Simmons died in the crash, while Martin bailed out and was rescued by Yugoslavian partisans.

On 4 March, the 332nd Fighter Group escorted the 49th BW to the Graz railway marshalling yards and later another mission took off to escort a reconnaissance Mosquito to Munich. At the end of February, the 302nd Fighter Squadron had ceased to exist and on 6 March it was officially scrapped. The pilots were assigned to the other units. The 332nd Fighter Group now consisted of three squadrons.

On 7 March, the 332nd Fighter Group escorted a P-38 to Munich, where it was supposed to take photographs, but was prevented by cloud cover. Thomas Hawkins, of the 100th Fighter Squadron, died that day when he lost control of his plane and crashed into some parked aircraft.

On 9 March, the 332nd Fighter Group provided escorts for three separate missions. Two were reconnaissance flights, one to Linz and the other to Munich. The last mission consisted of providing escorts for the 5th BW as it attacked the marshalling yards at Bruck, Austria. Three days later the recon flights would be repeated and the 47th BW was escorted to the Floridsdorf oil refinery in Austria.

Two hostile planes were spotted, but they were lost in the ground haze, when two P-51s went down to investigate. A bomber was being attacked by fighters, but when asked for the location, no replies came. Another bomber, a B-24 with two engines on fire, was escorted by two fighters to the Russian lines. The bomber was eventually lost in the clouds, but the bomber stated that he could remain in the air for fifteen more minutes, before the crew had to abandon the plane.

On 13 March, two reconnaissance flights took off. One went to Stuttgart and the other one went to Nurnberg. A P-51 took off ten minutes late and failed to link up with others. During his flight, the pilot came across a black FW-190 that wanted to engage him. He ditched his "tanks and turned in to attack. As [he] closed in he saw a second FW-190 coming down on him out of the sun from 4 o'clock above. P-51 split S'd and returned to base. The FW-190s followed P-51 to coast, but did not get within firing range."[4] This day the bomber-escort mission went to Regensburg railway marshalling yard, which would be attacked by the 5th BW. Two black FW-190s were seen, but they remained at a distance.

Four missions were planned for 14 March. Twice photo-escorts were needed for Mosquitos that went to Munich. The 100th and 301st Fighter

Members of the 332nd Fighter Group attending a briefing in Ramitelli, Italy, March, 1945. (Courtesy of Library of Congress)

Squadron escorted bombers of the 47th BW to the Varazdin railway marshalling yard and the nearby bridge. A single plane that had fallen behind, came across a bomber that returned early and provided an escort. Bombers of the 304th BW were unescorted and several planes were dispatched to provide them with an escort as well. Twenty-one airplanes

Tuskegee airmen exiting the parachute room, Ramitelli, Italy, March 1945. (Courtesy of Library of Congress)

of the 99th Fighter Squadron strafed targets on the Bruck-Leoben-Steyr railway line.

Nine locomotives and nine goods wagons were destroyed. Another nine locomotives, 127 goods wagons, thirty-seven flats cars, eight oil wagons, seven trucks on the flat cars, three railway stations, two railway buildings, a power station and a warehouse were left burning.

Harold Brown's plane was critically damaged in the strafing, as he himself recounted:

> If it had blown three seconds before, or even two seconds before, I might have time to pull up and at least to get away from the major part of that explosion. But it went over just

as I passed. The whole thing blew and I was caught right in the doggoned middle of it. All the debris that blew up, that came up in the air when it blew up, that hit the airplane and knocked off the oil line, damaged the engine and that's when the oil pressure … I lost all of the oil in the thing. The oil pressure was going to zero. The old temperature was swinging up to maximum. Then I lost all of my coolant. It came out of the engine. An inline engine without coolant doesn't run. Yes, it just freezes on you […] I went through it, rolled the airplane out. I came out of the explosion on my back. I rolled it out and came up. I looked around and there were all kinds of crap in the cockpit. But I said, "Hell, the thing is still flying. No sweat!" I said, "Boy, the gorgeous gun film pictures I took!" Because I was on the trigger all the way. I said, "Oh, man, this is going to be great when I get back!" Then a short while—I'm sure I'm talking about a matter of seconds, afterwards—that's when the gauges start going crazy on me, and I was pulling up trying to get altitude because I knew I was in trouble. Obviously. Then I lost all of the coolant […] I would bet that airplane ran about three or four minutes […] because I had pulled up and I was up about a thousand feet or so and Bill Campbell, Lucas and the guys who were waiting on it, they came around me and circled me and Campbell was waving at me looking at back. I looked back and saw smoke trailing out and of course, by then the engine instruments were telling me, you're in deep trouble here. So, I turned and I headed due east. I said, if this thing can just run for maybe fifteen, twenty minutes, I can get pretty close to the Russian lines and I just might get out of this. Well, it ran for no more than a minute or so.[5]

The propeller started windmilling, since there was no power to it. Desperate to get away, Brown released the canopy and pushed the stick forward, throwing him out of his plane.

After landing with his parachute, Brown stood there in the snow and watched the others as they circled him. For a brief moment he thought about escaping to the east, but two police constables were already closing in on him and brought him back to the village, where an angry mob of twenty-five to thirty people rapidly closed around him. A third constable arrived with his rifle.

Brown continues:

> The next thing I knew I saw the guy, and I heard him behind me and he was speaking in German, and I could hear him hit the bolt on his rifle, and that was very clear. There was this very rapid German discussion. It went on for a few seconds and the other two guys, I saw them drop their guns and they backed off into the mob and he motioned to me: Come. And I got in behind him, and he and I walked back, back up into the village about, I'm only guessing, an eighth of a mile, a quarter of a mile. It was just a short distance. The crowd was following us and he held the gun on the crowd while we backed up.[6]

After spending several hours in a barricaded café, they continued along the road. Harold Brown reflected on being saved from a beating or worse by the German constable, saying, "I was the enemy, but I wasn't his enemy at the time."[7]

Harold Brown was interned and spent the rest of the war as a POW. That day the 99th destroyed nine locomotives as well as nine box cars.

On 15 March, twice bombers were escorted by the 332nd Fighter Group: a mission to Yugoslavia and a mission by the 5th BW to Zittau. Out of the fifty-five planes that took off, forty-nine completed the mission. On the way back a lone B-17 was picked up and guided towards home.

On 16 March two reconnaissance flights took off. One Mosquito went to Munich and the other one went to Prague. William Price of the 301st Fighter Squadron, shot down a German Me-109 during a strafing mission, which cartwheeled into the ground. During the strafing, the 332nd Fighter Group destroyed seven locomotives, five box cars, a flak car, as well as three FW-190s and a JU-52 on the ground. Jimmie Wheeler died after striking a wire with his plane and crashing into the ground. The last mission was escorting bombers on that attacked a harbor in northern Italy.

Here are a few of the men who keep the 332nd Fighter Group in the air. Powerful engines of the group's P-51 Mustangs require expert mechanics, and these men are just that. (Courtesy of National Archives and Records Administration)

More reconnaissance escorts were flown in the days that followed, almost daily to a variety of destinations. At other times the 332nd Fighter Group provided escort for supply missions, delivering supplies to partisans in Yugoslavia.

On 19 March, bombers of the 55th BW were escorted to the railway yards at Muhldorf. One of the forty-five aircraft needed to return early due to a mechanical problem. The others continued with the mission. A jet-propelled aircraft was seen over the Brenner Pass, heading towards the south.

The next day bombers of the 304th BW were escorted to the Kralupy oil refinery in Czechoslovakia. Twenty-six aircraft took off and four returned early. Ten of the Mustangs linked up with the 304th BW and six needed to return early, due to a fuel shortage, while the remaining four stuck with the bombers. The remaining twelve aircraft linked up with the 49th BW and provided an escort to Linz. That day, Newman Golden, of the 99th Fighter Squadron, developed mechanical problems and went missing after jumping out of his aircraft. He was captured and spent the

Five pilots pose in front of a P-51 Mustang named "Skipper's Darlin". (Courtesy of Ike Skelton Combined Arms Research Library Digital Library)

rest of the war as a POW. On 21 March, the 47th BW was escorted to Neuberg, Germany. On the 22nd the mission of 20 March was repeated. Again the 304th was escorted and again it went to Kralupy oil refinery.

On 23 March, two waves of the 5th BW were escorted to the Ruhland oil refinery, Germany. During the mission Lincoln Hudson, of the 301st, developed engine trouble. He did not have enough altitude to cross the Alps so bailed out and was taken prisoner. He was beaten up and eventually brought to a POW camp, where he spent the rest of the war.

The longest mission

On 24 March, the 332nd Fighter Group would undertake its longest mission. The 5th BW would go to Berlin under escort of several fighter groups, the 332nd Fighter Group being one of them. Fifty-nine aircraft took off in the morning, five returned early. The 332nd took over escort duties from the P-38s of the 1st Fighter Group. When Commander

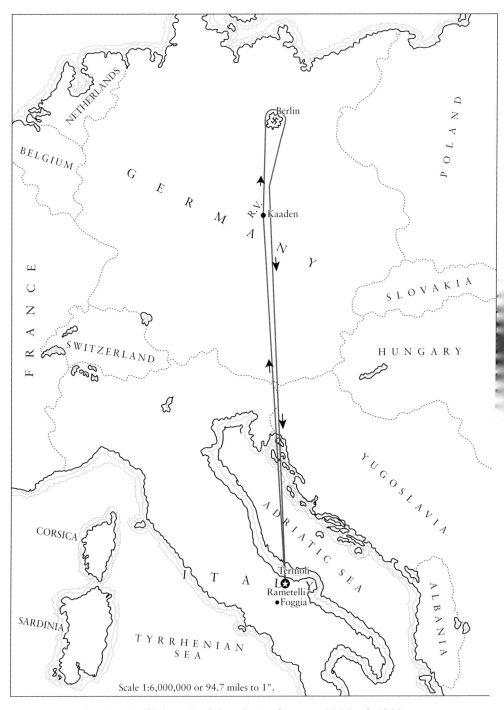

A map showing the flight path of the mission flown on 24 March 1945.

Davis' plane developed mechanical issues, Armour McDaniel took over. The expected escorts of the 31st Fighter Group did not show up, so the 332nd stayed with the bombers on their way to the target.

It swiftly became the fiercest encounter that the 332nd would experience. Several German planes were in the air, including the jet-propelled Me-262. Three pilots submitted claims for an aircraft shot down, including Roscoe Brown who downed an Me-262. According to his mission report:

> I sighted a formation of four Me-262s under the bombers at about 24,000ft. They were below me, going to North. I've peeled down on them to reward their rear but almost immediately I saw a lone Me-262, at 24,000ft, climbing at 90 degrees to me and at 25,000ft from me. I pulled up at him in a 15 degree climb and fired three long bursts at him from 2,000ft at 8 o'clock to him. Almost immediately the

Photograph shows (left to right) Roscoe C. Brown, Marcellus G. Smith, Colonel Benjamin O. Davis in Ramitelli, Italy, March 1945. (Courtesy of Library of Congress)

pilot bailed out from 24,500ft. I saw flames burst from the jet orifices of the E/A [enemy aircraft].[8]

Earl Lane and Charles Brantley also claimed an aircraft destroyed. Several other pilots claimed to have damaged German planes, such as Robert Williams of 100th Fighter Squadron:

> My wingman called in that two enemy aircraft were approaching from 5 o'clock high, so we turned into them. My wingman had one external tank still on and could not turn tightly. The two enemy aircraft fired at him and passed together below us. I split S'd and developed a high-speed stall, which put me a little out of effective range at about 1,500ft. The two enemy aircraft were in close formation until I fired two long bursts at the rearmost enemy aircraft. I fired 30 degrees deflection shots at seven o'clock. I noticed pieces of the enemy aircraft passing my ship. The enemy aircraft fell out of formation to the rear. I broke off the attack when my wingman called for help.[9]

The mission was not without casualties, however. Armour McDaniel was shot down and became a POW. Ronald Reeves and Robert Robinson both returned due to a lack of fuel and went missing. Later it was discovered they were killed. Leon Spears was low on fuel and, together with James Mitchell, set out for the Soviet frontline. However, while Mitchell made to safety, Leon Spears fell just short of it.

As he recounted about his experience:

> I was hit by German 88 guns during a mission over Berlin at 32,000ft. That's almost six miles straight up! There was no way I could get back to Italy and make it over the Alps, so I had to crash land "Kitten" in Poland. I would have to be at least 18,000ft to cross the mountains. I knew by the way my engine was sounding that I would be no way near 18,000ft to make it home.
>
> I turned 90 degrees west toward Poland and I landed near this river. The Germans were on one side of the river

Marcellus G. Smith and Roscoe C. Brown tend to a P-51. (Courtesy of Library of Congress)

and the Russians were on the other side. Between the two of them, they shot my plane to pieces. You see, when the P-51 Mustang is flying directly at you it looks like an Me-109 from certain angles. While I was flying down this river, I could feel shells hitting the plane. I said to myself, well, I'm on this side of the river so the shells got to be coming from those Russians. Once they saw that I was an American they stopped firing at me. As I remember, I saw myself coming toward this runway. I said to myself that if I let the wheels down, I could probably make a pretty good landing. I decided not to land because I did not want the enemy to use the plane. As I was in the process of putting the wheels up, I hit the ground. I did not have enough power to work the hydraulics.

Surprisingly, it was Germans that came right away in a car. There were two officers and three enlisted men in Nazi helmets and they had their guns pointed right at me. I put my hands in the air and they motioned for me to come close. They could see that I had a .45 pistol. They made motions that they wanted that .45 on the ground, which I did. It seems to me that they were trying to be as nice as they could because they knew that the war was coming to an end for them, so they did not want to get too cruel. The Germans did know about the Geneva Convention which dealt with war crimes. They did not want to be involved in any war crimes. They sat me in the car and drove to their headquarters. I was interrogated by a German official who asked if I could speak English. He asked me where did I come from. I told him. "I'm sorry, I can't tell you. I can tell you, my name. rank and serial number." I spoke: "You know the Geneva Convention, don't you." He said, "Yes," whenever he would ask me something. I would mention the Geneva Convention then he would say, "I'm sorry I ask," and that was it. They knew full well that any information they could get would be useless for them. I was only with them for three days.

The Russians were in Poland and they were advancing about twenty-five to thirty-five miles a day. At about the third day I heard all this ripping and roaring, and the building was shaking and everything. All the glass was out of the windows, but I pulled a board off a window area and the first thing I saw was this huge Russian tank. There were forty or fifty guys surrounding it going through the town blowing up buildings. This scared me because I thought that they would blow this building up that I was in. I was screaming and hollering to them and a guy that looked like a Russian officer looked up and saw me. When I saw him looking at me, I had an A-2 flight jacket on with a large

American flag on the back. I put my back to the window so he could see it and I could hear him yell. "American! American!" He came up and gave me a big bear hug![10]

Spears was liberated and returned to the 332nd Fighter Group on 10 May.

Despite the losses incurred, the mission was very successful and for its performance over the skies of Berlin, the 332nd Fighter Group would be awarded the Distinguished Unit Citation. The citation reads as follows:

On March 23, 1945, the group was assigned the mission of escorting heavy bombardment type aircraft attacking the vital Daimler-Benz tank assembly plant at Berlin, Germany. Realizing the strategic importance of the mission and fully cognizant of the amount of enemy resistance to be expected and the long range to be covered, the ground crews worked tirelessly and with enthusiasm to have their aircraft at the peak of mechanical condition to ensure the success of the operation.

ON MARCH 24, 1945, 59 P-51 type aircraft were airborne and set course for the rendezvous with the bomber formation. Through superior navigation and maintenance of strict flight discipline the group met the bomber formation at the designated time and place. Nearing the target approximately 25 enemy aircraft were encountered which included Me-262s which launched relentless attacks in a desperate effort to break up and destroy the bomber formations.

Displaying outstanding courage, aggressiveness, and combat technique. the group immediately engaged the enemy formation in aerial combat. In the ensuing engagement that continued over the target area, the gallant pilots of the 332nd Fighter Group battled against the enemy fighter to prevent the breaking up of the bomber formation and thus jeopardizing the successful completion of this vitally important mission. Through their superior skill and determination. the group destroyed three enemy aircraft, probably destroyed three, and damaged three. Among their claims were eight of the highly rated enemy jet-propelled aircraft with no losses sustained by the 332nd Fighter Group.

LEAVING the target area and en route to base after completion of their primary task, aircraft of the group conducted strafing attacks against enemy ground installation and transportation with outstanding success but the conspicuous gallantry. Professional skill, and determination of the pilots, together with the outstanding technical skill and devotion to duty of the ground personnel, the 332nd Fighter Group has reflected great credit on itself and the armed forces of the United States.

There was little rest for the remainder of the 332nd Fighter Group. The day after they had flown a fifteen-hour mission, they again provided escorts for bombers as well as reconnaissance flights. The 332nd Fighter Group provided escorts for the 49th BW on a mission to Prague. During the mission several fighters were ordered to guide early returning bombers home. During the mission, a Soviet PE-2 was seen, rocking its wings to indicate that it recognized the American planes – the incident again being a sign of how the Third Reich was pressed from all sides. However, Mustangs from another group did not recognize the aircraft and shot it down in a fatal case of "friendly fire". No parachutes were seen.[11]

On 26 March, the 5th BW was escorted to Wiener Neustadt railway marshalling yards. The bombers had gone off course due to the bad weather, but the 332nd Fighter Group guided them over the target and on the way home.

Although no missions were flown on 27, 28, and 29 March, there was still a casualty to mourn. A taxiing plane dropped its external fuel tank, which burst into flames near the tent Roland Moody was in. He died from his injuries.

On 31 March, the 332nd performed a fighter sweep over the area of Munich, Germany. Forty-seven airplanes took off and four returned due to mechanical issues. As Colonel Davis recounted:

We finished March in a blaze of glory: on the last day of the month, I led a fighter sweep of the Munich area, during which we encountered seventeen German aircraft

Deputy Group Commander George S. "Spanky" Roberts with photographer Toni Frissell, at Ramitelli, Italy, March 1945. (Courtesy of Library of Congress)

conducting a low patrol above an enemy airdrome thirty miles east of Munich. Not one escaped unharmed. We destroyed thirteen, probably destroyed three, and damaged one—our largest number of enemy aircraft destroyed in the air on any single day.[12]

The 99th Fighter Squadron was assigned to strafe the western sector, the 301st Fighter Squadron was assigned the center, while the 100th Fighter Squadron strafed the eastern sector. As the 99th was about to descend on a target, they were attacked by six enemy aircraft: five Me-109s and an FW-190. They took down all of them. The 100th Fighter Squadron engaged the eleven enemy aircraft. At first a group of five enemy aircraft were spotted. Later they were joined by another group of six. The German planes had little chance, and the attrition of the Luftwaffe is seen in their performance. The hostile aircraft fought aggressively, but did not work together and each tried to take on the 100th Fighter Squadron on their own, resulting in the destruction of several aircraft, including seven FW-190s, and two Me-109s. Another FW-190 was a probably destroyed and an Me-109 damaged.[13]

Arnett Starks was hit by anti-aircraft artillery and was declared dead a year and a day later. Frank N. Wright got into a tight turn and was unable to get out of it in time, due to the low altitude of his plane. He died in the crash. Clarence Driver went missing, but survived the war.

The last months

On 1 April, forty-five pilots escorted the 47th BW to St. Polten, Austria, where they bombed the railway marshalling yard. The fighters of the 301st went ahead of the bombers and then turned west, performing a fighter sweep in the area of Wels and Linz. While flying, they spotted four FW-190s below them. The P-51s descended upon them, but it was an ambush. The FW-190s were shadowed by two other FW-190s and ten other German fighters waited above them to close the trap. The Germans attacked aggressively, although the Americans prevailed. Three of the fighters were shot down by Harry Stewart, and Charles White shot down two of them. Carl Carey, John Edwards, James Fischer, Walter Manning, and Harold Morris also shot down one.

Fischer's plane was shot while pursuing the enemy over the airfield and while flying over Yugoslavia, he was hit again; he bailed out and was rescued by partisans. William Armstrong was killed in combat.

In a gruesome twist of fate, the Tuskegee Airmen were exposed to lynching even in Europe. Allied airmen could become the victim of German officials or members of the state police wishing to exact revenge. After Walter P. Manning's plane had been shot down, he jumped out of his aircraft and drifted towards the ground, where he was taken prisoner. He was locked up at the Linz-Hörsching air base, where, around 03:30 am, two men – most likely Luftwaffe political officers – arrived

Edward C. Gleed next to a wingtank with two unidentified people in Ramitelli, Italy, March 1945. (Courtesy of Library of Congress)

with forged orders to take him away. Due to his skin color and Nazi propaganda, he was an easy target. What transpired next is unclear, but Manning was found the next day hanging from a lamppost with a sign. Manning is the only known Tuskegee Airmen to be lynched during the Second World War in Austria.

On 2 April, the 304th BW was escorted, attacking the marshalling yard at Krems. The reconnaissance mission of that day, to Munich, was attacked by a single Me-262. On 5 April, the 5th BW was escorted to Udine airfield, while the Luftwaffe never took off to defend their airbase. It was an indication that the Luftwaffe was spent, having run low on aircraft, fuel, and pilots. On 6 April, the 304th BW attacked the railway marshalling yards at Verona and Porta Nuova under escort of the 332nd Fighter Group.

On 7 April, the 5th BW bombed bridges in Northern Italy and again escorts were provided by the 332nd Fighter Group. One plane briefly landed in Yugoslavia, before the pilot and the plane returned to Ramitelli. Ferrier White went missing that day while flying over the Adriatic Sea.

On 8 April the 332nd Fighter Group flew escort for the 5th BW. The bombers attacked in three waves. The target was the railway bridge at Campodazzo, Italy. No resistance was encountered, although one bomber ditched in the Adriatic Sea. On 9 April the Mustangs of the 332nd Fighter Group were escort for bombers of the 5th and 304th BW. The target was Bologna, Italy. The next day the mission was repeated.

Four P-51 Mustangs flying in formation in Ramitelli, Italy, March 1945. (Courtesy of Library of Congress)

On 11 April, the 332nd Fighter Group escorted bombers of the 304th BW to Ponte Gardena, attacking the railway bridge. Two damaged bombers were escorted to safety by four P-51s. The recon mission went to Munich.

Bombers of the 47th BW were escorted to Casara railroad bridge on 12 April and bombers of the 49th BW to St Veith. Two P-51s collided during this mission. James L. Hall was captured after bailing out and Samuel Leftenant was killed. On 14 April, the 332nd Fighter Group escorted Halifaxes that dropped supplies.

William A. Campbell and Thurston L. Gaines in Ramitelli, Italy, March 1945. (Courtesy of Library of Congress)

The 332nd Fighter Group strafed targets between Munich, Salzburg, Linz, Prague and Regensburg on 15 April. Jimmy Lanham attacked an Me-109 and destroyed it. Morris E. Gant went missing and Thurston Gaines was shot down and taken prisoner by the Germans.

On 16 April, three C-47s were escorted by four P-51s of the 332nd Fighter Group to Yugoslavia. The 49th BW and the 55th BW were escorted to Bologna that day by the 332nd Fighter Group. It was also the day that Franklin Roosevelt, the US president, died. On 17 April the 332nd Fighter Group escorted the 5th and 304th Fighter Groups to the same target. The next day the 304th was again escorted to Bologna. It

An unidentified Tuskegee airman sitting on the wing of a P-51 in Ramitelli, Italy, March 1945. (Courtesy of Library of Congress)

was originally intended that the 5th BW would be escorted, but confusion prevented a correct rendezvous and the 304th BW was escorted instead.

Forty-seven P-47s of the 332nd Fighter Group escorted the 304th BW on 19 April. They were split in three groups. One group of nineteen escorting a group of bombers to Wels and another one of sixteen to Pucheim. The remaining seven conducted a fighter sweep. No hostile planes were encountered in the air, but they did find a location where a group of around forty Me-163s were seen.

On 20 April, the 49th BW and 55th BW were escorted by the 332nd in their attack on railroad bridges in Northern Italy. Meanwhile, back in the United States, Wendell Pruitt – one of the pilots that had engaged and sunk the German torpedo boat – died in an accident. As Colonel Davis wrote about the accident:

> I recall the case of Capt. Wendell Pruitt, one of our best flight leaders. After he completed his seventy combat missions he went home and was reassigned as a flying instructor at TAAF. Shortly thereafter I received a rather agitated letter from him asking that I request his immediate reassignment to Italy. The day after I had answered his letter assuring him that I had already requested him, I received a letter from Agatha informing me that she had read in the *Pittsburgh Courier* of Pruitt's death in an aircraft accident.[14]

On 21 April, the 332nd Fighter Group escorted the 49th BW to the Attang/Pucheim railway marshalling yards. The group failed to rendezvous with the bombers, due to the inclement weather, but linked up with them on the return. Leland Pennington radioed to the others that he would return to base alone. He never arrived and was recorded as missing, being later declared killed. His remains were never recovered. A fighter sweep was conducted and lastly two bombers were escorted to Yugoslavia, where they dropped supplies for the local partisans.

The 332nd Fighter Group performed an armed reconnaissance in northern Italy on 22 April. The next day the bombers of the 55th BW and the 304th BW were escorted by the 332nd Fighter Group on missions to Padua and Cavarzere. Two waves of P-51s took off to escort the bombers. Sixteen planes of the first force looked for targets between

Colonel Benjamin O. Davis Jr., half-length portrait, wearing flight gear, standing next to a P-51. (Courtesy of Library of Congress)

Verona, Marostica, Padua, Cavarzere, Staghella, and Legnana. A railway line was strafed and one car and a factory damaged. Hugh White was hit by flak and he managed to climb high enough to bail out safely.

On 24 April two waves of escorts were provided by the 332nd Fighter Group. They escorted the 47th BW and the 49th BW to their targets and back.

On 25 April four groups of eight aircraft took off for an armed reconnaissance mission of the area around Verona. A convoy was spotted and engaged, before the red crosses on the targets were noticed. Three reconnaissance missions were flown that day. Two of those missions encountered a German plane, but neither was engaged.

"Escape kits" being distributed to fighter pilots at air base in Ramitelli, Italy, 1945. (Courtesy of Library of Congress)

On 26 April the 332nd Fighter Group made their last kills. A P-38 was escorted by six P-51s. Photographs were taken of Linz, Prague and Amstetten. An airplane was sighted by three P-51s, but it was a friendly Mosquito. While climbing, a formation of five Me-109s was spotted, they rocked their wings to appear friendly. Once the P-51s were among them, two of the Me-109s pulled up as if they wanted to dive. An American pilot opened fire and shot at one of the German aircraft, sending it down in flames. Three of the Me-109s went for the deck, but were caught by the two other P-51s. Two fighters remained and they were shot down after a short chase. Thomas Jefferson claimed a kill

A Tuskegee Airman looks at planes in the sky. (Courtesy of Library of Congress)

and a probable. Richard Simmons, Jimmy Lanham each claimed one as well. Back at Ramitelli, escorts were provided for the 47th BW and 55th BW. In five waves the P-51s took off, escorting the bombers to Casarsa and Malcontenta.

The last days were anxious. It was obvious that the war would soon be over and for the 332nd that was indeed the case, as they had flown their last mission on 30 April. Four planes escorted a P-38 to Bolzano, Italy.

Also on this day, Adolf Hitler and his wife Eva Braun committed suicide in a bunker in Berlin. Missions might have been scheduled for 1 May, but no reports of them have been located. On 7 May the German forces surrendered unconditionally.

Four P-51 Mustangs of various fighter groups flying over the Alps. From rear to front: 31st, 52nd, 332nd and 325th Fighter Group. (Courtesy of National Archives and Records Administration)

Chapter 6

Tuskegee Airmen at home and in the Pacific

The Freeman Field Mutiny

Although the battle in Europe was over, the fight continued in the Pacific against Imperial Japan. Likewise, the battle against Jim Crow also continued. For the Tuskegee Airmen who served only in the US, the biggest battle was the mutiny at Freeman Field.

While the 332nd Fighter Group fought in the Mediterranean, replacement pilots were trained in the US. Furthermore, in January 1944 a segregated bombardment group was established, the 477th Bombardment Group. It consisted of the 616th, 617th, 618th, 619th Bombardment Squadron. They flew with B-25 Mitchell bombers. The unit was trained under the command of Colonel Robert Selway, who endorsed segregation policies. The soldiers suffered under his leadership. The 477th Bombardment Group moved through several stations. The unit never made it into combat, but it did need to fight.

As Colonel Davis recounted from the experiences:

> Other black combat returnees, however, were unhappy with their assignments after returning to the States. The AAF reassigned most of them to TAAF or Walterboro, and they felt that their experience, rank, and talents were being neglected or misused. Colonel Parrish later cited the surplus of black officers at TAAF and his inability to use them effectively; AAF Headquarters, which preferred to confine its black officer problem to as few bases as possible, continued reassigning black combat returnees to TAAF and

162

Walterboro. Some of these returnees, notably Lee Rayford, Herbert Clark, Bill Campbell, and Louis Purnell, after having completed one combat tour with the 99th, were so dissatisfied with their status as returnees that they joined the 332nd for a second tour and the "easier" job of combat flying. The fact that they preferred risking their lives overseas to the uselessness of their jobs in the States gives some idea of how little genuine responsibility they were given.[1]

Racial trouble was brewing. The senior officers were white, and although some of them had served in combat, others had not. The Black officers, including veterans from Italy, were placed in subordinate positions, much to their frustration. At the base in Indiana, ironically named Freeman Field, Colonel Robert Selway had divided the officers' clubs along racial lines and covered it up by claiming that there was a distinction between the Black trainees and the white instructors. However, all the Black officers were trainees, while all the white officers were instructors. This

A group of Tuskegee Airmen with Roger Terry in the center at Tuskegee Army Airfield, December 1944. (Courtesy of National Archives and Records Administration)

was a clear violation of army regulations, which stated that all army officers could attend all officers clubs on all bases. Club number 2 was not accessible for the Black officers, but on the night of 5 April, a coordinated non-violent attempt was made to "integrate" the club.

Lieutenants Marsden Thompson and Shirley Clinton entered the club and were arrested after refusing to leave. They were soon joined by Roger Terry. More officers attempted to enter and refused to leave. That first night, thirty-six officers were taken away into custody. The next night, twenty-five more Black officers attempted to enter the segregated officers club and were arrested. In total, sixty-one Black officers were held in custody.

On 9 April Selway issued a base regulation, outlining who could use what recreational facilities on the base. To ensure all officers had knowledge about this order, the Black officers were required to sign a written version of it; 101 of the approximately 400 present refused to do this.

The 101 officers were arrested for insubordination, because they refused to acknowledge the order. They were flown back to Godman Army Airfield, Kentucky, on 13 April and placed under house arrest. The notoriety of the case forced the Airforce in a complicated position. The War Department, the Black press and members of congress were all watching. Senior command within the army eventually ordered the release of all officers, except for three which had used force to gain entry. A court martial was held, and two were acquitted. Only Roger Terry was fined $150 for forcing his way past an MP. In the 1990s the charges were dismissed. After the court martial, Colonel Selway was replaced by Colonel Davis, who assumed command on 24 June.

However, Davis had a tough task ahead of him. Not only did he need to get the 477th back on track, he also had a multitude of other tasks:

> I had to deal with the problem of finding family housing for the officers and airmen who had returned with me from Italy. […] All our married people, about sixty couples, were housed under extremely crowded conditions in two barracks buildings at Godman. The building Agatha and I lived in had two bathrooms, one for men and one for women, but the other building had only one bathroom for

two floors full of people, and they had to devise a guard system to indicate whether the bathroom was being used by men or by women at any particular time. In both buildings the rooms, which had been designed for single occupancy, were more like cells. In the other building they had been partitioned off from one another with wooden panels that went only halfway to the ceiling, so there was no privacy. It was an absolutely disgraceful situation, and a terrible way to treat combat veterans who had fought one war and were soon to be on their way to fight another. I shall never forget nor forgive this shameful treatment of our veterans and their families by officers of the US Army, who were fully aware of the situation and yet allowed it to continue. To add insult to injury, our palatial quarters were adjacent to barracks occupied by Italian prisoners of war under the control of the Fort Knox command.[2]

The 477th BG was redesignated the 477th Composite Group on 22 June 1945, when the 99th Fighter Squadron became assigned to it. The 616th and 619th BS were inactivated. The 477th consisted of both fighters and bombers. The pilots started training for deployment in the Pacific. The P-51s were replaced by P-47s, although they never made it into combat.

On 6 August 1945, the United States dropped an atomic bomb on Hiroshima, and three days later on Nagasaki. Shortly afterwards, on 15 August, the surrender of the Japanese Empire followed and the Second World War came to an end. A new world would wait for everyone.

With the war over, the need for manpower diminished. This was also seen in the 477th Composite Group, there the 618th BG was inactivated on 8 October 1945. In February 1946, just sixteen B-25 and twelve P-47Ns remained. In March 1946 the group was transferred to Lockbourne Field, near Columbus, Ohio. They were the only all-Black airbase in the Army Air Force. After arrival, it was the intention of Colonel Davis to make the base the best in the Army Air Force. In 1948 there was a statement in an inspection report that said the base could serve as a model for other bases. In May 1947, the bombers were put away and the 332nd Fighter Group became itself once more. It was downsized even further, becoming the 332nd Fighter Wing.

In May 1949, the newly established US Air Force would hold its first continental gunnery meet. Teams from every fighter group took part in it. There were six categories: air-to-air gunnery at 10,000ft and 20,000ft, skip bombing, rocket-firing, dive-bombing and strafing. The scores of each team on each event would be averaged out to determine who was

Captain Alva Temple, Lieutenant Harry Stewart, and Lieutenant James Harvey. (Courtesy of National Archives and Records Administration)

the winner. On behalf of the 332nd Fighter Wing, Captain Ava Temple and First Lieutenants James H. Harvey and Harry T. Stewart Jr. would compete. In the end, the 332nd Fighter Wing won the competition for "conventionally powered" aircraft. On 30 June, the 332nd Fighter Wing would be inactivated.

Service in the Pacific

Besides the Tuskegee Airmen mentioned above, serving as single-engine pilots or twin-engine pilots, there was a lesser-known group. The liaison pilots. These pilots flew as artillery liaisons for the 92nd and the 93rd Infantry Division or the Black artillery battalions. The 92nd Infantry Division was employed in Italy and the 93rd Infantry Division served in the Pacific. Both units consisted of Black American soldiers and had white or mixed officer cadres.

The liaison pilots usually flew in L-4 Grasshoppers, also known as Piper Cubs, and performed reconnaissance as well as artillery coordination. Due to their height, the small aircraft could see where the artillery hit and easily redirect the fire. These adjustments were necessary to provide an accurate artillery strike on the target. The small aircraft were also employed in a variety of other ways, such as delivering mail or messages between units. One of these pilots wrote extensively about his experiences, Welton I. Taylor, giving an impression of what this service was like. Although these pilots did not serve in combat, as the unarmored and unarmed planes were poorly suited as combatants, the pilots still faced danger. This could be due to environmental hazards, which formed a greater risk in the Pacific as well as the mechanical issues. These factors took a toll on the equipment and material, which resulted in Welton Taylor crashing more than once. Welton Taylor returned after the Second World War to the US and had a distinguished career as a scientist.

Chapter 7

Desegregating the military

"There would be nothing for us to look forward to if someone
did not stay in to give young boys a chance at flying after
we have fought and died for the opportunity."

George Watson.[1]

On 25 July 1948, Executive Order 9981 was issued by President Harry
S. Truman, who previously had met Dale White and Chauncey Spender.
In that order all discrimination based upon "race, color, religion or
national origin" was abolished in the United States Armed Forces. It led
to the integration of the American military service. However, that was
still years into the future.

The homecoming of Black American soldiers was different to what
they might have anticipated. Not all of them received the heroes'
welcome that their white countrymen received. After experiencing life in
the Pacific or Europe, the Black veterans returned with more confidence
and new skills. They were ready to assert themselves, but there were
white people waiting to put them back in their place.

When veteran Eugene Bell returned from the war, he refused to work
for his previous employer, a white farmer in Amity County, Mississippi.
Instead, Bell worked at the farm of his father-in-law. This angered his
previous employer, who threatened Bell. Things escalated on the night
of the night of 25 August 1945, when Bell was driving a car with other
passengers. Another vehicle started to follow them and suddenly opened
fire. Bell pulled over and was taken from the car by white men, who beat
him so severely that his skull was crushed – then they shot him in the head.[2]

There were other incidents of senseless violence such as the lynching
at Moore's Ford bridge, Georgia and the beating of Isaac Woodard. On
12 February 1946, Sergeant Isaac Woodard, a Black man and veteran of

the war in the Pacific, boarded a Greyhound bus in Georgia to go home to his family in North Carolina. He would never reach his destination.

When at a rest stop, Woodard asked the bus driver if there was time to use the restroom. After an argument, the driver allowed it and once finished Woodard returned to his seat. When the bus stopped in Batesburg, South Carolina, the driver contacted local white police, which included Sheriff Lynwood Shull. Woodard was taken from the bus and beaten by Batesburg policemen in an alley.

Woodard was then put in jail on the accusation of drinking beer on the bus. Over the course of the night, Woodard was mistreated by the police, including Shull. They punched him with their fists and jabbed a billy club in his eyes.

Two days later a doctor was sent to Woodard and he was eventually brought to a hospital in Aiken, South Carolina. Suffering from amnesia, and not knowing where he was, it took three weeks, before he was located by his family. The case was covered by the Black press and it caused much uproar. The government in South Carolina was reluctant to pursue the case and President Truman ordered the Justice Department to start an investigation. The resulting trial was a farce and the defense attorney even shouted racial slurs at Woodard. After Woodard told his version of the events, Shull claimed that Woodard had threatened him with a gun and he used his billy club in self-defense. The all-white jury cleared Shull of any wrongdoing, despite his admission of blinding Woodard.[3]

Another incident involved two couples, George Dorsey, a veteran of the war in the Pacific, and his wife Mae Murray, and Roger Malcolm and his wife Dorothy – who was seven months pregnant; Dorsey and Malcolm worked as sharecroppers for J. Loy Harrison. On 11 July 1946. Roger Malcom allegedly stabbed Barnette Hester, a white man. On 25 July, Harrison, Dorothy, and the Dorsey couple went to pick up Roger Malcolm from jail after posting the $600 bail. On the road back, over a less-travelled path, the road was blocked by a group of fifteen to twenty armed white men. The white men took the two Black men out of the car. When one of the women recognized one of the assailants, both women were also tied to a tree alongside their husbands. The four people were then shot sixty times at close range by the mob.[4]

The lynching was covered in the national press and President Truman ordered a federal investigation. However, Harrison could not identify any of the attackers. No charges were filed and 'the last mass lynching in America', as the case became known, still remains unsolved. These are but a few incidents in a multitude of similar happenings.

The return of the Black veterans caused much tension and lynchings were a reminder of the racial differences in American society. The lynchings were abhorred by Black, and also many white Americans. President Truman was disgusted with what was happening in the country, even saying:

> My stomach turned over when I learned that Negro soldiers, just back from overseas, were being dumped out of army trucks in Mississippi and beaten. Whatever my inclinations as a native of Missouri might have been, as President I know this is bad. I shall fight to end evils like this.[5]

Ernest W. Roberts, a friend of Harry Truman, commented on Truman's actions, when he was striving towards equal rights. Roberts was displeased with the way things were going and wrote: "Harry, let us, let the South, take care of the niggers, which they have done. And if the niggers do not like the southern treatment, let them come to Mrs. Roosevelt."[6]

Harry Truman was severely displeased with this letter and the way in which his friend recommended him to solve the issue. On 18 August 1948, his reply included the following paragraph:

> When the mob gangs can take four people out and shoot them in the back, and everybody in the country is acquainted with who did the shooting and nothing is done about it, that country is in pretty bad fix from a law enforcement standpoint. When a Mayor and a City Marshall can take a Negro Sergeant off a bus in South Carolina, beat him up and put out one of his eyes, and nothing is done about it by the State authorities, something is radically wrong with the system.[7]

Truman refers directly to the lynching at Moore's Ford Bridge and the blinding of Isaac Woodard. Truman disagreed with the treatment of his citizens and took serious action against it, using his executive powers. He established "The President's Committee on Civil Rights" in 1946 as a direct response to the violence against Black veterans. On 29 June 1947 he was the first president to address the NAACP at an annual convention. On 25 July 1948 Truman issued Executive Order 9981, ending segregation in the US Armed Forces.

Crew Chief Marcellus G. Smith working on an airplane. (Courtesy of Library of Congress)

Coming home

The war had been a long and tiring experience for many of the pilots. They were glad it was over and they could go home. As mentioned however, not all of them received the same welcome as white servicemen had received. As Joe Gomer recounted of his return in December 1944:

> I think I was the only person of color in all the thousands of people. We came back on the SS *America*. We had to wait for a troop ship. It came time to board ship and I was with a group of officers. There weren't a lot of officers there, but I did meet Sgt. Hill from my hometown, if you can imagine that. But the officers went first, naturally. There was a short, fat, redneck captain standing up on this little box. […] I was a first lieutenant. When he got to me, he just looked and ordered me to the end of the line. Now I was a combat veteran. I'm on my way home, a war hero. And that guy probably had not seen a day of combat in his life. Well, the second time he ordered me to the end of the line, I wanted to come home; I picked up my duffel bag and bell pack and went to the end of the line, behind everybody.[8]

This photograph shows Woodrow Crockett from the 332nd Fighter Group signing the Form One Book, indicating any discrepancies of aircraft prior to take off. (Courtesy of Library of Congress)

The Second World War did accelerate social changes however. As Felix Kirkpatrick recounted, "at an altitude of 35,000ft, with flak bursting around you and Focke-Wulfs snapping at your heels, race prejudice vanishes."[9] He remembered being hugged by bomber crews for saving their lives. During his service, he has seen bombers being torn apart or crashing down in flames, while fighters slipped out of formation or just disappeared.

Within their local communities, the Tuskegee Airmen were seen as heroes, because they had overcome both Jim Crow and the German enemies. The men came home, proud of their service as well as conscious of their rights. Many of them had experienced a life and liberty that they would never have achieved otherwise. They were determined to keep their earned rights, as well as strive for more.

British soldiers and Black citizens

A comparison can be made between the Black American and the Black British airmen. For Black British citizens, the situation was at first much the same. Initially only British people of 'pure European descent' could enter the service. The color bar was lifted in October 1939, approximately two months after the invasion of Poland by Nazi-Germany.[10] It took some time before Black volunteers were accepted. Following the Battle of France and during the Battle of Britain, in the second half of 1940, the Royal Air Force suffered many casualties and the RAF started to actively recruit in the West Indies. Men from the Caribbean were actively recruited, and to a lesser extent volunteers from West Africa were welcomed.

The arrival of Black soldiers resulted in some conflicts relating to the status quo. After arriving at RAF Cranwell for officer training, William Strachan – a recruit from Jamaica – was assigned a batman. He described their first meeting:

> The batman was a very smooth Jeeves type and exactly the kind of character I had been led to expect. Meanwhile, I was just a little colored boy from the Caribbean. When I first met him, I instinctively called this English batman, "Sir". "No, Sir," the Batman hastily corrected me, "It is I who call you Sir."[11]

In October 1942, a group of Jamaican aircrew were brought to Canada aboard an American ship. After embarking at Kingston harbor, the US crew sent the Black passengers below deck. After setting up in a bunch of empty bunks, the passengers were sent two decks further below by a white officer, staying in the hold of the ship. Regardless of their being volunteers and destined to be aircrew of an Allied nation, as far as the American sailors were concerned, they were just Black people and the American racial attitudes prevailed.

While West Indian volunteers still encountered racism and discrimination, it seemed to be more the result of personal prejudices and less systemic than the racial discrimination of the Black American pilots.

As the war was nearing its end, the need for new soldiers diminished and the recruitment of Black volunteers was stopped. Reinstating the previous color bar was proposed by the RAF and the Air Ministry. This met with resistance from the Colonial Office, that claimed it would be impossible to carry out the proposal. Black soldiers had served during wartime, why would they be incapable of serving in peacetime?

The Air Ministry appeared to comply, but issued verbal instructions to dismiss Black volunteers. A memorandum, dated 16 August 1945, by the Air Chief Marshall Sir John C. Slessor, Air Member for Personnel on the Air Council, reveals the abhorrent mindset of some of those involved. He writes about the "unsuitability of a gentlemen with a name like 'U-be' or 'Ah Wong'", or who "looks as though he has just dropped out of a tree" for a service in an arm as prestigious as the RAF.[12]

When the war was over, the Black Caribbean soldier returned home. However, it seems that their contribution to the war, was rapidly forgotten. To prevent painful reminders of their sacrifices, it seems that the RAF kept silent about their contribution. It is only in recent years that more attention is given to the contribution of West African and Caribbean volunteers in the Second World War.

One veteran recalled that during the war he did not face any racism, but it was only after the war that the problems started to arise. Harry McCalla from Jamaica said, "It was all right until the English became aware of color. About 1955 or '56, I'd say. I had difficulty getting a flat then. There were so many immigrants coming in."[13]

Unlike the USA, the UK did not practice any segregation. Black volunteers served in a multitude of positions, including navigators or rear gunners in a bomber, such as Lincoln Lynch. A Jamaican, Lynch served in the Royal Air Force during the Second World War; he was as a gunner in No 102 Squadron RAF and is credited with shooting down a German aircraft. Racist white Americans were shocked by the relaxed racial attitudes of the British people. There were several benefits for the British army. People, regardless of skin color, could employ their talents where they were most effective. Meanwhile, the armed services had an expanded pool of manpower to use. Additionally, integration leads to a more efficient utilization of resources, and so the British Armed Forces fought more effectively.

Legacy and debates

Out of the fighter groups in the 15th Air Force, the 332nd is the most well-known. There are many (auto)biographies, articles, histories, internet pages. Some of the more sensational articles have grand claims about the Tuskegee Airmen, such as that they never lost a bomber.

The bomber escort missions could consist of various duties. It could consist of escorting the bombers to the destination – penetration escort; or return from the target – withdrawal escort; or escort over the target, or combination of these. During missions many fighter groups would cover a multitude of bomber groups.

Although the claim has been made that the 332nd Fighter Group never lost a bomber, this is not true. A close examination of the losses experienced by the bombers escorted by the 332nd Fighter Group has revealed that several bombers under their escort had been lost.

Likewise, people might have the idea that the Tuskegee Airmen all flew red-tailed P-51s. However, the experiences of the Tuskegee Airmen are much broader than their service as bomber escorts starting in July 1944. While indeed these are some of the most famous missions, the 99th Fighter Squadron flew a large part of its combat career in the P-40 Warhawk, being employed as a ground-attack aircraft, a role it performed very well.

In recent years attention has been devoted to the Tuskegee Airmen, giving them long overdue honor. At military bases and in communities in the US, streets are named after Tuskegee Airmen, and memorials, including statues, are established at important sites to commemorate the them.

An unidentified Tuskegee airman sitting on the nose of a P-51 in Ramitelli, Italy, March 1945. (Courtesy of Library of Congress)

Memorials are also erected in Italy, in the vicinity of the former Ramitelli airfield. On 16 July 2023, a monument consisting of a stone marker commemorating the 332nd Fighter Group was unveiled. In a nearby village a was mural revealed which depicts Benjamin O. Davis, Jr. standing in front of several P-51s. The aircraft is instantly recognizable due to its distinctive red noses and tails.

Soaring to glory

After the war was over, many of the Tuskegee Airmen continued to serve in the United States Air Force. Others returned to civilian life,

Pilot Newman C. Golden scanning the skies in Ramitelli, Italy. (Courtesy of Library of Congress)

where they had success in a variety of endeavors. All of them continued to fight for an integrated society.

William Momyer, who had written the damning report of the 99th Fighter Squadron, continued to serve in the United States Air Force. He retired from the USAF in 1973 and died in 2012.

Charles Dryden continued to serve in the United States Air Force. During the war in Korea, he flew as a reconnaissance pilot. In 1962 he retired with the rank of lieutenant-colonel. He passed away in 2008.

Luther Smith retired from the air force in 1947. He acquired an engineering degree at the university of Iowa in 1950 and continued working as an aerospace engineer. He died in 2009 and is buried at Arlington National Cemetery. His injuries and recovery caused his right leg to be seven inches shorter than his left leg. It resulted in a permanent disability.

Walter "Ghost" Lawson, who had acquired his nickname from his miraculous survival of the crash in the AT-6, where Richard Dawson lost his life, died in 1952 in an airplane accident. When the B-50 bomber was landing, it crashed and exploded. Lawson and four others perished in the crash.[14]

Harold Brown, who had been taken prisoner in March 1945, experienced another frightening moment during his captivity. While being transported from one camp to another, he was strafed by Allied fighters. He recounts these experiences:

> Oh my God. That was the most terrifying thing I have ever experienced. Particularly that first time. I mean, it was absolutely terrifying. You could hear the bullets. You could hear the airplane coming over. And there's no place to run. No place to hide. Nothing […] And we were all on the floor. And I don't even know how long the train was. I don't know if it was an engine with ten cars, twelve cars, fifteen cars or what. But it felt like there was only one car and that was the car that you were in and all the bullets were being directed towards your one car. That was not the case. But that's what it felt like. That was the most terrifying thing up to that point that I've ever experienced. You were scared as hell.[15]

The train eventually stopped in a tunnel and no one in Brown's group was hurt. He was eventually liberated. Harold Brown continued to serve in the Air Corps, also serving in Korea, and eventually retiring in 1965 as a lieutenant-colonel. He earned a doctoral degree and worked as an administrator at Columbus State Community College. He retired in 1986 and died in January 2023.

As for Joe Gomer, he stayed in the Air Force after the order for integration had come. Not all was well yet, however. As Joe Gomer recalled:

When we were assigned after integration to Langley Air Force Base, we integrated that base. And later on, they put another one of our officers who was high ranking, he was a supply squadron CO, but his wife would not do anything or go anywhere without my wife. I think I was probably a captain by then.[16]

Joe Gomer retired in 1964 as a major from the United States Air Force. Afterwards he worked for the US Forest Service. Joe Gomer retired in 1985. He was also invited for special events:

The 459th Heavy Bomb Group, the B-24s, had their 13th annual reunion in St Paul. In 1993, I think. Anyway, they heard there was a Red Tail pilot in the area, so my wife and I were invited down, and we spent two days with them.

Photograph shows three Tuskegee Airmen looking skyward, Ramitelli, Italy, March 1945. (Courtesy of Library of Congress)

At the big banquet, since I wasn't on the program, but they did give me a few minutes to speak, afterward some of the guys came up with tears just shaking my hand and saying, "We waited fifty years to thank you guys for saving our butts." We never had any interactions [during the war]. We shared the skies, but that's all.[17]

Joe Gomer passed away in 2013.

William Green, who had to bail out on 13 October 1944 after helping to blow up an ammunition dump in Yugoslavia, returned to the 332nd Fighter Group and was even decorated with the Partisan Medal.[18] Green continued to serve and fought in the Korean War; he passed away on 24 November 1974.

Leon Spears, who had been captured by the Germans and liberated by the Russians, also fought during the Korean War. During one of these missions, his younger brother George, was shot out of the sky. It devastated him and he returned to the US, where he worked for the Postal Service. He died on 12 May 2008.

Alexander Jefferson had been captured in August 1944. He was eventually liberated by American soldiers and continued to serve in the Air Force reserve. He retired in 1969 and continued working as an assistant principal in Detroit, Michigan. From this he retired in 1979. He celebrated his 100th birthday in 2021 and died on 22 June 2022.

Colonel Benjamin O. Davis continued his service in the United States Air Force, rising to the rank of major general, and retired in 1970. While in retirement, he was promoted to general. Davis passed away in 2002. His life is a testament to what people can achieve if they are determined to succeed.

Literature list

100th Fighter Squadron, Special Account, Earl S. Sherard.

100th Fighter Squadron, War Diary, February 1944.

100th Fighter Squadron, War Diary, March 1944.

100th Fighter Squadron, War Diary, March 1944.

301st Fighter Squadron, Historical Records, March 1944.

301st Fighter Squadron, War Diary, February 1944.

301st Fighter Squadron, War Diary, March 1944.

301st Fighter Squadron, War Diary, May 1944.

301st Fighter Squadron, War Diary, May 1944.

302nd Fighter Squadron, War Diary, June 1944.

332nd Fighter Group, Narrative Mission Report 119, 16 November 1944.

332nd Fighter Group, Narrative Mission report 179, 16 February 1945.

332nd Fighter Group, Narrative Mission Report 204, 1 March 1945.

332nd Fighter Group, Narrative Mission report 219, 13 March 1945.

332nd Fighter Group, Narrative Mission Report 248, 25 March 1945.

332nd Fighter Group, Narrative Mission Report 252, 31 March 1945.

99th Fighter Squadron, Daily Operations Report, 23 August 1944.

99th Fighter Squadron, Outline History, May – Oct 1943, Part II.

99th Fighter Squadron, War Diary, December 1943.

99th Fighter Squadron, War Diary, February 1944.

99th Fighter Squadron, War Diary, April 1944.

99th Fighter Squadron, War Diary, March 1944.

99th Fighter Squadron, War Diary, November 1943.

99th Fighter Squadron, War Diary, October 1943.

Army War College, Employment of Negro Man Power in War (1925).

Bucholtz, Chris, *332nd Fighter Group: Tuskegee Airmen* (Oxford, 2007).

CAF Rise Above, 'George Thomas McCrumby', https://cafriseabove.
  org/george-thomas-mccrumby/ .

CAF Rise Above, 'Maurice V. Esters', https://cafriseabove.org/maurice-v-esters/.

Cooper, Robert T., The 33rd Fighter Group: "Fire from the clouds" (Maxwell AFB, 1988).

Correspondence Between Harry S. Truman and Ernie Roberts (1948), Harry S. Truman.

Craig Lloyd, *Eugene Bullard, Black Expatriate in Jazz-Age Paris* (Athens, 2006) 61-62.

Davis Jr., Benjamin O., *American: An Autobiography* (Washington , 1991).

Department of the Interior, *Moton Field: Tuskegee Airmen Special Resource Study* (Atlanta, 1998).

Dryden, Charles W., *A-Train: Memoirs of a Tuskegee Airmen* (Tuscaloosa, 1997).

Equal Justice Initiative, *Lynching in America: Targeting black veterans* (Montgomery, 2019).

Fort Worth Star-Telegram, *Airmen killed in crash are named*, 27 February 1952.

Handleman, Philip, and Harry T. Stewart Jr*., Soaring to Glory: A Tuskegee Airman's Firsthand Account of World War II* (Washington, 2019) 63.

Haulman, Daniel, *Tuskegee Airmen Chronology* (expanded edition, 2011).

Haythornthwaite, Philip, *The World War One Sourcebook* (London, 1998).

Historical Record, 99th Fighter Squadron, January 1944.

Historical Records, 302nd Fighter Squadron.

Historical Studies Branch USAF Historical Division, *Combat crew rotation* (Maxwell Air Force Base, 1968) 1.

History, 301st Fighter Squadron, February 1944.

History, 301st Fighter Squadron, January 1944.

History, 301st Fighter Squadron, July 1943.

History, 301st Fighter Squadron, June 1943.

History, 301st Fighter Squadron, May 1943.

History, 301st Fighter Squadron, November 1943.

Jefferson, Alexander, *Red Tail Captured, Red Tail Free: Memoirs of a Tuskegee Airmen and POW* (New York, 2017).

LITERATURE LIST

Johnson, Mark, *Caribbean Volunteers at War: The Forgotten story of the RAF's 'Tuskegee Airmen'* (Barnsley, 2014).

Luce, Steve W., *86th Fighter Group in WWII* (Hamilton, 2007).

Milton R. Brooks, Statement, 22 July 1944.

Mollo, Andrew, *The Armed Forces of World War II: Uniforms, Insignia and Organization* (Hong Kong, 1981).

National Park Service, 'Harry S Truman and Civil Rights', https://www.nps.gov/articles/000/harry-s-truman-and-civil-rights.htm, updated 18 August 2021.

Official German Broadcasts: North American Affairs, 'U.S. Negro Pilots make Poor Showing', 22 January 1944.

RAF Museum, 'Robbie Clarke: Britain's First Black Pilot', https://collections.rafmuseum.org.uk/story/robbie-clarke-britains-first-black-pilot/#object-modal-0

Richardson, Virgil, and Ben Vinson III, *Flight: The Story of Virgil Richardson, A Tuskegee Airman in Mexico* (New York, 2004).

Saylor, Thomas, "Oral History Project World War II Years, 1941–1946 – Harold Brown" (2004). Oral History Project: World War II Years, 1941–1946. 9, https://digitalcommons.csp.edu/oral-history_ww2/9.

Saylor, Thomas, "Oral History Project World War II Years, 1941–1946 – Luther Smith, Jr." (2005). Oral History Project: World War II Years, 1941–1946. 75, https://digitalcommons.csp.edu/oral-history_ww2/75.

Saylor, Thomas, "Minnesota's Greatest Generation Oral History Project: Part I: Interview with Joseph Gomer", http://collections.mnhs.org/cms/display?irn=10803255#transcript.

Smithsonian, Benjamin O. Davis Jr. Collection – Distinguished Unit Citation, March 24, 1945.

The Daily Bulletin, 'Pilot saved life by being unconscious', 27 August 1945.

The Michigan Chronicle, 'Award Given for Mission October, 1944', 3 November 1945.

The Michigan Chronicle, 'How Lieut. Thos. Malone was Injured By Land Mine', 4 March 1944.

The Omaha Guide, 'Ethiopian flyer spikes threat of war', 5 October 1935.

The Pittsburgh Courier, '322nd Veteran Back In U.S.', 18 November 1944.

The Pittsburgh Courier, '332nd, Back in States, Asks: 'Give us Civilian Air Jobs'', 27 October 1945.

The Pittsburgh Courier, 'Fliers Narrate How Germans Hound Them; One Death', 16 October 1943.

The Pittsburgh Courier, 'Indiana Youth Bests Deadly Focke-Wulf In Air Battle Above Clouds Over Sicily', 10 July 1943.

The Pittsburgh Courier, 'Lone Mustang Flies On P-38 Lightning Mission', 24 March 1945.

The Pittsburgh Courier, 'When Will "99th" Move?', 20 February 1943.

The Sphinx, 'Brother in 99th Fighter Squadron Makes Supreme Sacrifice', 1943.

Time Magazine, 'Army & Navy – Experiment Proved?' 20 September 1943.

Wings of History Air Museum, 'Tuskegee Airmen', https://www.wingsofhistory.org/tuskegee-airmen/.

Endnotes

Chapter 1: Pre-Second World War

1. Philip Haythornthwaite, *The World War One Sourcebook* (London, 1998) 112.
2. Craig Lloyd, Eugene Bullard, Black Expatriate in Jazz-Age Paris (Athens, 2006) 61-62.
3. RAF Museum, 'Robbie Clarke: Britain's First Black Pilot', https://collections.rafmuseum.org.uk/story/robbie-clarke-britains-first-black-pilot/#object-modal-0.
4. Army War College, Employment of Negro Man Power in War (1925) 1.
5. Army War College, Employment of Negro Man Power in War, 4.
6. Army War College, Employment of Negro Man Power in War, 2.
7. Andrew Mollo, *The Armed Forces of World War II: Uniforms, Insignia and Organization* (Hong Kong, 1981), 115.
8. *The Omaha Guide*, 'Ehtiopian flyer spikes threat of war', 5 October 1935.
9. Davis Jr., Benjamin O., *American: An Autobiography*, 27.
10. Davis, *American*, 28-29.
11. Charles W. Dryden, *A-Train: Memoirs of a Tuskegee Airmen* (Tuscaloosa, 1997) 87.
12. Dryden, *A-Train,* 89.
13. *The Pittsburgh Courier*, 'When Will "99th" Move?', 20 February 1943.

Chapter 2: Service in Africa and Sicily

1. Dryden, *A-Train,* 119-121
2. 99th Fighter Squadron, Outline History, May – Oct 1943, Part II.
3. Dryden, *A-Train,* 129.

4. Robert T. Cooper, The 33rd Fighter Group: "Fire from the clouds" (Maxwell AFB, 1988).

5. Dryden, *A-Train,* 124.

6. Dryden, *A-Train,* 126.

7. *The Pittsburgh Courier*, 'Indiana Youth Bests Deadly Focke-Wulf In Air Battle Above Clouds Over Sicily', 10 July 1943.

8. Dryden, *A-Train,* 138.

9. *The Pittsburgh Courier,* 'Fliers Narrate How Germans Hound Them; One Death', 16 October 1943.

10. *The Pittsburgh Courier,* 'Fliers Narrate How Germans Hound Them; One Death', 16 October 1943.

11. *The Pittsburgh Courier,* 'Fliers Narrate How Germans Hound Them; One Death', 16 October 1943.

12. 99th Fighter Squadron, Outline History, May – Oct 1943, Part II.

13. *The Pittsburgh Courier,* 'Fliers Narrate How Germans Hound Them; One Death', 16 October 1943.

14. 99th Fighter Squadron, Outline History, May Oct 1943, Part II.

15. Dryden, *A-Train,* 145 – 146.

16. 99th Fighter Squadron, War Diary, October 1943.

17. 99th Fighter Squadron, War Diary, October 1943.

18. 99th Fighter Squadron, War Diary, December 1943.

19. *The Sphinx*, 'Brother in 99th Fighter Squadron Makes Supreme Sacrifice', 1943.

20. *The Michigan Chronicle*, 'How Lieut. Thos. Malone was Injured By Land Mine', 4 March 1944.

21. *Time Magazine*, 'Army & Navy – Experiment Proved?' 20 September 1943.

22. Davis, *American*, 103-104.

23. Philip Handleman and Harry T. Stewart Jr*., Soaring to Glory: A Tuskegee Airman's Firsthand Account of World War II* (Washington, 2019) 63.

24. Davis, *American*, 107.

Chapter 3: Making progress

1. History, 301st Fighter Squadron, May 1943.

2. History, 301st Fighter Squadron, June 1943.

3. History, 301st Fighter Squadron, July 1943.
4. History, 301st Fighter Squadron, November 1943.
5. Historical Records, 302nd Fighter Squadron.
6. Historical Records, 302nd Fighter Squadron.
7. 99th Fighter Squadron, War Diary, November 1943.
8. 99th Fighter Squadron, War Diary, December 1943.
9. 99th Fighter Squadron, War Diary, November 1943.
10. Official German Broadcasts: North American Affairs, 'U.S. Negro Pilots make Poor Showing', 22 January 1944.
11. Historical Record, 99th Fighter Squadron, January 1944.
12. Historical Record, 99th Fighter Squadron, January 1944.
13. Historical Record, 99th Fighter Squadron, January 1944.
14. Davis, *American*, 114.
15. 99th Fighter Squadron, War Diary, February 1944.
16. 99th Fighter Squadron, War Diary, February 1944.
17. CAF Rise Above, 'George Thomas McCrumby' https://cafriseabove. org/george-thomas-mccrumby/.
18. *The Pittsburgh Courier*, '322nd Veteran Back In U.S.', 18 November 1944.
19. 99th Fighter Squadron, War Diary, March 1944.
20. 99th Fighter Squadron, War Diary, March 1944.
21. 99th Fighter Squadron, War Diary, March 1944.
22. 99th Fighter Squadron, War Diary, April 1944.
23. 99th Fighter Squadron, War Diary, April 1944.
24. 99th Fighter Squadron, War Diary, June 1944.
25. Davis, *American*, 119.
26. Davis, *American*, 120.

Chapter 4: The 332nd Fighter Group in Italy

1. Historical Records, 302nd Fighter Squadron.
2. History, 301st Fighter Squadron, January 1944.
3. Historical Records, 302nd Fighter Squadron.
4. Davis, *American*, 115.
5. 301st Fighter Squadron, War Diary, February 1944.
6. 301st Fighter Squadron, War Diary, February 1944.

7. Thomas Saylor, "Minnesota's Greatest Generation Oral History Project: Part I: Interview with Joseph Gomer", http://collections. mnhs.org/cms/display?irn=10803255#transcript.

8. 100th Fighter Squadron, War Diary, February 1944.

9. 100th Fighter Squadron, War Diary, March 1944.

10. History, 301st Fighter Squadron, February 1944.

11. Davis, *American*, 118.

12. 100th Fighter Squadron, War Diary, March 1944.

13. 100th Fighter Squadron, War Diary, March 1944.

14. 100th Fighter Squadron, War Diary, March 1944.

15. 301st Fighter Squadron, Historical Records, March 1944.

16. 100th Fighter Squadron, War Diary, March 1944.

17. 301st Fighter Squadron, War Diary, March 1944.

18. 301st Fighter Squadron, War Diary, March 1944.

19. Virgil Richardson and Ben Vinson III, Flight: The Story of Virgil Richardson, A Tuskegee Airman in Mexico (New York, 2004) 61.

20. 301st Fighter Squadron, War Diary, May 1944.

21. 302nd Fighter Squadron, Historical Records, March 1944..

22. 100th Fighter Squadron, War Diary, April 1944.

23. 301st Fighter Squadron, War Diary, May 1944.

24. 100th Fighter Squadron, Special Account, Earl S. Sherard.

25. 301st Fighter Squadron, War Diary, May 1944.

26. 302nd Fighter Squadron, War Diary, June 1944.

27. Davis, *American*, 122-123.

28. Department of the Interior, Moton Field: Tuskegee Airmen Special Resource Study (Atlanta, 1998) 114.

29. *The Pittsburgh Courier*, 'I saw Captain Tresville Die And Aided In The Sinking Of A Destroyer', 9 December 1944.

30. *The Pittsburgh Courier*, 'I saw Captain Tresville Die And Aided In The Sinking Of A Destroyer', 9 December 1944.

31. CAF Rise Above, 'Maurice V. Esters', https://cafriseabove.org/ maurice-v-esters/

32. Steve W. Luce, 86th Fighter Group in WWII (Hamilton, 2007) 136.

33. Historical Studies Branch USAF Historical Division, Combat crew rotation (Maxwell Air Force Base, 1968) 1.

34. Thomas Saylor, "Oral History Project World War II Years, 1941–1946 – Harold Brown" (2004*). Oral History Project: World War II*

Years, 1941–1946. 9, https://digitalcommons.csp.edu/oral-history_ww2/9.

35. Mollo, *The Armed Forces of World War II*, 245.
36. Milton R. Brooks, Statement 22 July 1944.
37. *The Daily Bulletin,* 'Pilot saved life by being unconscious', 27 August 1945.
38. Alexander Jefferson, *Red Tail Captured, Red Tail Free: Memoirs of a Tuskegee Airmen and POW* (New York, 2017) 59.
39. 99th Fighter Squadron, Daily Operations Report, 23 August 1944.
40. Thomas Saylor, "Oral History Project World War II Years, 1941–1946 – Luther Smith, Jr." (2005). *Oral History Project: World War II Years, 1941–1946.* 75. https://digitalcommons.csp.edu/oral-history_ww2/75.
41. Saylor, "Oral History Project World War II Years, 1941–1946 – Luther Smith, Jr.".
42. Saylor, "Oral History Project World War II Years, 1941–1946 – Luther Smith, Jr.".
43. Saylor, "Oral History Project World War II Years, 1941–1946 – Luther Smith, Jr.".
44. Saylor, "Oral History Project World War II Years, 1941–1946 – Luther Smith, Jr.".
45. Saylor, "Oral History Project World War II Years, 1941–1946 – Luther Smith, Jr.".
46. 332nd Fighter Group, Narrative Mission Report 119, 16 November 1944.
47. Davis, *American*, 131.
48. Davis, *American*, 131.

Chapter 5: Death of the Luftwaffe

1. 332nd Fighter Group, Narrative Mission report 179, 16 February 1945.
2. *The Pittsburgh Courier,* 'Lone Mustang Flies On P-38 Lightning Mission', 24 March 1945.
3. 332nd Fighter Group, Narrative Mission Report 204, 1 March 1945.
4. 332nd Fighter Group, Narrative Mission report 219, 13 March 1945.

5. Saylor, "Oral History Project World War II Years, 1941–1946 – Harold Brown".
6. Saylor, "Oral History Project World War II Years, 1941–1946 – Harold Brown".
7. Saylor, "Oral History Project World War II Years, 1941–1946 – Harold Brown".
8. Smithsonian, Benjamin O. Davis Jr. Collection – Distinguished Unit Citation, March 24, 1945.
9. Smithsonian, Benjamin O. Davis Jr. Collection – Distinguished Unit Citation, March 24, 1945.
10. Wings of History Air Museum, 'Tuskegee Airmen', https://www.wingsofhistory.org/tuskegee-airmen/.
11. 332nd Fighter Group, Narrative Mission Report 248, 25 March 1945.
12. Davis, *American*, 134-135.
13. 332nd Fighter Group, Narrative Mission Report 252, 31 March 1945.
14. Davis, *American*, 128.

Chapter 6: Tuskegee Airmen at home and in the Pacific

1. Davis, *American*, 128.
2. Davis, *American*, 144-145.

Chapter 7: Desegregating the military

1. *The Pittsburgh Courier*, '332nd, Back in States, Asks: 'Give us Civilian Air Jobs'', 27 October 1945.
2. Equal Justice Initiative, Lynching in America: Targeting black veterans (Montgomery, 2019) 43.
3. Equal Justice Initiative, Lynching in America, 42.
4. Equal Justice Initiative, Lynching in America, 27.
5. National Park Service, 'Harry S Truman and Civil Rights', https://www.nps.gov/articles/000/harry-s-truman-and-civil-rights.htm, updated 18 August 2021.
6. Correspondence Between Harry S. Truman and Ernie Roberts (1948), Harry S. Truman.

ENDNOTES

7. Correspondence Between Harry S. Truman and Ernie Roberts (1948), Harry S. Truman.
8. Saylor, "Interview with Joseph Gomer".
9. *The Weekly Review,* "Vet of Seventy Airmissions, Negro tells of saving pilots," 20 January 1945
10. Mark Johnson, *Caribbean Volunteers at War: The Forgotten story of the RAF's 'Tuskegee Airmen'* (Barnsley, 2014) 36.
11. Johnson, *Caribbean Volunteers at War,* 61.
12. Mark Johnson, *Caribbean Volunteers at War: The Forgotten story of the RAF's 'Tuskegee Airmen'* (Barnsley, 2014) 178.
13. Johnson, *Caribbean Volunteers at War,* 85.
14. *Fort Worth Star-Telegram,* Airmen killed in crash are named, 27 February 1952.
15. Saylor, "Oral History Project World War II Years, 1941–1946 – Harold Brown".
16. Saylor, "Interview with Joseph Gomer".
17. Saylor, "Interview with Joseph Gomer".
18. *The Michigan Chronicle*, 'Award Given for Mission October, 1944', 3 November 1945.

Index

INDEX

INDEX